BACK ON TOP

BACK ON TOP
Fearless Dating
After Divorce

Ginger Emas

life

Guilford, Connecticut
An imprint of The Globe Pequot Press

To buy books in quantity for corporate use
or incentives, call **(800) 962–0973**
or e-mail **premiums@GlobePequot.com.**

life

GPP Life is an imprint of The Globe Pequot Press.

Project manager: Imee Curiel
Interior designer: Sheryl P. Kober
Layout artist: Kim Burdick

Library of Congress Cataloging-in-Publication Data is available on file.

ISBN 978-1-59921-545-7

Printed in the United States of America

10 9 8 7 6 5 4 3 2 1

This book is dedicated to all the women who are finding the courage and wit to date again . . . who are getting out there to like and love and be loved, especially after a divorce, a bad breakup, or another relationship-from-hell. It's sometimes scary to be alone; but it's always scarier to be in something that's not true to who you are. I'm with you. I applaud you. I'll help you return your wedding gifts.

Disclaimer

The names and places and even some of the stories in this book have been changed or altered to protect the privacy and reputations of the people who shared their stories with me. Don't even try to guess who's who because I used an ancient form of Pig Latin to disguise and distract and you will think you know who I'm talking about but you will be completely wrong and it might mess up your own mojo or karma next time you see that person (or worse, judge her/him) so why not just chill out and read and laugh so hard you almost pee in your pants and you start to snort a little. After all, in today's world, what's better than a really good laugh, especially at my expense?

Contents

Introduction
Back on Top

THE DAY I GOT MARRIED, I WAS DELIGHTED WITH THE possibilities—a lifetime partner to honor, cherish, and have babies, minivans, and power tools with. I think that every bride who walks down the aisle is not only dreaming of her future but also privately saying to the world: *See? Someone finds me wonderful enough to have spent two months' salary on a ring, put on a rented tux and those black patent-leather shoes, and decided to live with me forever— even when I'm PMSing.*

But the main thing that I, personally, was secretly thrilled with was that I would never, ever have to go on a date again. Especially not a first date, the singularly most anxiety-producing part of dating.

Well, I was wrong.

Two years ago, after thirteen years of marriage, I became the first person in my family's history—all the way back to my great-great-great-grandparents in Siberia, Russia—to get a divorce. The divorce itself wasn't so bad. Mutual. Amicable. Friendly, even. I told my ex I was really glad I had married him because he is great to be in a divorce with.

It's the post-divorce dating that I just wasn't up for yet. It takes a while to feel like you're back on top. But I knew I'd get there. After all, it's my favorite position.

So, for a while, I just didn't. Date, that is. Instead I took kick-boxing and Pilates and digital photography and salsa dancing (all listed in the catalogs under "Classes for the Newly Divorced"), and I channeled my energy into these healthy activities.

But one can only dance alone for so long.

So I started to tiptoe into the dating world again. Only this time there was a whole new world out there: online dating, speed dating, Lock and Key parties.

I discovered that people don't necessarily date—they hook up or have friends-with-benefits. People spend hours getting to know each other before they ever meet or even talk on the phone. Instead they text and IM (and if I have to tell you that *IM* means "instant message," don't worry—that's how far behind I was when I first started dating. Feel free to just skip to the good parts).

There were rules I'd never heard of: A guy who is interested in a girl never calls before three days, but doesn't wait longer than five. Women who date younger guys are called "cougars," and I don't think there is anything remotely complimentary about this branding. Younger men who like older women refer to them as MILFs—and we are supposed to be flattered. (You will be.) If you call the person you've been dating for the past week and your call goes straight to voice mail, it means something other than he is not available. The list of rules (and the ones I broke on a nightly basis) is actually quite lengthy.

Being a quick learner, however, I went from crawling to walking to running very quickly. In the two years since I have been divorced, I have been on approximately eighty-seven dates. This alone makes my friends' jaws drop and has anointed me some kind of default dating expert. Combine that with the fact that I have been dating since I was fifteen (minus the decade or so that I was married) and during those years I had likely been on 500 dates—100 of them *blind* dates—well, that should make me some kind of reality-show survivor.

But it is my post-divorce dating that gives me my true dating cred. *Because it took being married to cure me of the near-desperate desire to be married that consumed most of my twenties.* And believe me, dating with that goal in mind—to get married—is the most prevalent cause of disastrous dating. It causes us to date people we wouldn't even sit next to on the subway. It causes us to stay in relationships that are completely wrong and possibly dangerous to our health and self-esteem. God forbid we give up on a relationship in which we've invested two or five or ten years because he is the wrong guy. "What, and start all over?"

> It took being married to cure me of the near-desperate desire to be married that consumed most of my twenties.

Let me tell you, *starting over* is one of the most beautiful phrases in the English language, if you can just embrace it and buy enough mint chocolate chip ice cream to get you through the first three weeks of lonely nights. It's hard to pick up the phone and sob or plead when you are stuffing green ice cream into your mouth.

With this dating crown thrust upon me, I have road-tested a lot of the various forms of dating—the methodologies, the ages, the occupations, the parties, the Web sites. And I found that I really enjoy simply *dating*. I have met some incredible men, boys, and women. (For clarity, I only date the men, but I have been to parties where the most fun and fabulous people by far were the women—I'm talking, like, ten to one. It did occasionally give me pause to consider if I was playing for the right team.)

I have learned what I like and dislike in a man and what my must-haves are. I think every woman should have a dating checklist to refer to—a Manfile that includes notes about past dates, boyfriends, and husbands—so she is not tempted to consider a guy who embodies one or more of her non-negotiables. Of course, it's not garlic—even armed with my Manfile, I sometimes attract undesirables.

Not surprisingly, while I was out road-testing I made a whole new group of friends who were as unaware of the modern rules, online etiquette, and secret guy-code as I was. I heard hundreds of dating war stories, fairy tales, and dates-from-hell. I would regale my friends with tales from my own crypt and we would laugh and cry and say this would make a great book someday.

Well, someday is here.

A lot of the stories and advice are from my own dating adventures. But I also consulted a bevy of assistant dating experts (read: people I know who are also out there making up the rules and putting their lives online). The majority of people I spoke with were women, but I quickly learned that this was a great way to meet guys and at the same time see if they could tell a good story. (That's one of my must-haves.) The names have been changed to protect the guilty—and me.

I tried to categorize my stories by the topics I thought you'd want to know about most. This wasn't as easy as it sounds, because I could have categorized them by level of idiocy and come up with an entirely different book.

Maybe you will find an answer to your own questions here. Or maybe you will determine that I am Darwinizing dating, and the fact that I am out there dating gives you a considerable leg up on the competition.

And one thing before we continue: At the very least, you've got to really learn how to use your cell phone if you're going to date in today's world. That means how to text, block your number, identify callers. Because the first thing you'll learn in this new dating world is that nobody writes down his or her phone number anymore, and sometimes handing a guy your business card is handing him too much information. Instead, you'll just put your number into a guy's cell phone. You can input your name as anything you want— "girl from last night," your real name (first name only), whatever. Maybe he'll even remember it when he looks you up on his cell to give you a call. He did say he'd call, right?

> At the very least, you've got to really learn how to use your cell phone if you're going to date in today's world.

Oh, which reminds me. I'd like you to stop, right now, and call this number: 415-228-0207. It's called Rejection Hotline and it's pretty funny. It's the number you give to guys who ask you for your number but to whom you would *never* give your number and this is nicer than saying, *Not if you were the last breathing man on Earth.* In any case, you have to leave as soon as you give it so you won't be around when he calls it. And if he doesn't get it, then he doesn't have a sense of humor and you were right to give him this number in the first place.

It's kind of juvenile—okay, it's *very* juvenile—but I think it can also be its own dating litmus test. I was telling the hostess at my favorite midtown pizza place about the number—well, actually, I was shouting the number to her from across the dining room (attractive ladylike behavior, I know). A guy at the counter piped up and said, "Hey, I know that number! That's my ex-girlfriend's number."

I asked him out immediately.

Okay, we've wasted enough time when you could have had a date already. Let's get started. Go put on your first-date outfit.

What? You don't have a first-date outfit? This is going to be more challenging than I thought . . .

Chapter 1

We're All in This Together

THERE ARE MORE THAN A MILLION OF US EVERY YEAR DOING this dating-after-divorce thing. We're everywhere. At the gym. At the mall. On the soccer field. Maybe I've seen you. Maybe I've talked to you. I'm the one with two left feet dancing next to you in salsa class. I'm the one who spun the bowl right off the wheel in beginning pottery. Weren't you the one I laughed with last week at ladies' night about the eighty-year-old guy on the dance floor having more fun and getting more women than any two forty-year-olds?

We're in this together.

We want to meet nice guys but we have a hard time believing they're out there. We want to date but we're not sure we want to get married again. We want to try another relationship but we don't know how it will fit with our kids, our work, our lives, our ex.

We're scared . . . not all the time, but all of us, sometimes. We spend an inordinate amount of time thinking about how we don't measure up—we're not young enough or pretty enough, we're not tall enough or smart enough, our boobs are too small, our butts are too big, we have too many kids, too little time.

> We're scared . . . not all the time, but all of us, sometimes.

But every once in a while we whisper to ourselves in the mirror, "Hey, you look good. You're funny. You're kind. You're smart. You're strong." Why is that a whisper? That should be a shout! And I'm right there next to you, *not* shouting . . . Why are we like that?

I know in my heart that we all have something to offer to the dating world, to our next relationship, and the one after that.

Someone Whose Baggage Goes with Mine

Yes, we all come with baggage—some of us are dragging those heavy-duty sleep-away-camp duffel bags; some of us come with a matching set of Louis Vuitton steamers. It doesn't matter. Like the chick in *Rent* says, "I'm just looking for someone whose baggage goes with mine." And someone who can carry his own trunk. Uphill. And maybe even offer to carry mine once in a while.

Of course, if we're going to date, we're going to have to leave the baggage at home and go out there with just our purse and a lip gloss and enough cash to cover our drink. It's okay. Maybe if we don't take it with us on every date, our baggage won't keep us from enjoying the trip.

And girl, we've been to some wild destinations, haven't we? I've probably been where you are and you've probably been where I'm going. And we're all in this together.

I loved my husband with everything I had, and it still didn't work out. The first time I seriously thought about divorce was eleven years before I did anything about it. Okay, maybe I stayed a few years too long. Maybe you did, too. Of course, you probably didn't begin couples therapy the week after you got engaged and continue for 5,000 more sessions like I did. But it took me a long time to get over the fact that I said I'd stay forever. And in the end I think I stayed just exactly as long as I was supposed to.

It's Awfully Bright in Here

Maybe you think you didn't try everything you could have to keep your marriage together. I think about that, too. I never did that *Cosmopolitan* magazine tip from the 70s that suggested "greet your husband at the door wearing only Saran Wrap," but I'm fairly certain he would have seen right through that. We were pretty far past Saran Wrap.

I remember feeling that I needed a really big reason to get divorced. You know, a reason like, "He's been living a double life and has another family in California." My reasons didn't seem worthy enough to warrant a divorce. When I spoke them out loud, they sounded small. Our issues were actually pretty big, but from the outside we looked like a normal, happy family. On the inside, we were anything but.

I kept asking God to show me a sign. Have you ever done this? Asked the world or Spirit or Mother Nature to show you a sign? I asked a dozen times. Okay, a hundred. I kept asking and didn't realize that the world had been answering, showing me

> My reasons didn't seem worthy enough to warrant a divorce.

signs all the time. And not just little signs—great big 1,000-watt road signs. And I kept going around them or pushing through them or tripping over them. Finally, one day God shined this bright glaring fluorescent sign in my face. I tried to look away, of course. I was an expert at that, after all. But He held it there until I finally looked. And He said, "Is this sign big enough for you? Can you see yourself at all in this beam?" And I guess that's what it took for me to, *um,* see the light.

Damn If We Won't Try

I don't want to keep ignoring signs, do you? That's what's so cool about being women . . . and having been girls. We all went through pretty much the same things growing up, on one side of adolescence or the other. We understand. We talk. We laugh. We cry. We help simply by letting each other know that we are not alone. We're not embarrassed; hell, we're survivors and proud of it and damn if we won't try to save one more woman from one more bastard . . . or just one more bad relationship . . . just by being there to lend an ear, an eye, a shoulder.

Even so, I felt guilty. Maybe you did, too. I kept saying to myself, *How could I do this to my son?* And then one day (that day with the big fluorescent God-sign) it hit me: How could I *not* do this *for* my son?

After all those years of hurt and confusion and dashed hopes, that one sentence finally made sense.

We're all in this together. We have been lost, uncertain, scared. I have felt that I made a mistake, and then made another one. I have felt sad, tired, and really, really alone. Even when I was married. Maybe mostly when I was married.

I don't feel alone now—even though I am by myself more than ever before. Of course, I talk to myself more than ever before, and I can't remember half the things I've said. Especially once I get to the top of the stairs to retrieve whatever it was I was talking to myself about going to get.

The thing is, we're *not* alone. We have children and siblings and friends and colleagues and parents. All of whom *I* felt deserved an answer, an explanation, their wedding gifts returned. They didn't. They didn't ask. They supported.

> **I don't feel alone now—even though I am by myself more than ever before.**

Here We Are

And now we are at this point in our lives, together. I have Wednesday nights and every other weekend to myself, when my son is with his dad. I have blind dates and social dates. I have Girls' Nights Out. I have second thoughts.

I have been scared witless and I have been braver than I ever dreamed I could be—sometimes at the same time.

I have felt drained. Betrayed. Confused. I have also felt strong, inspired, and more authentic than ever before. I have felt happy—gleeful, even. Sometimes I feel sexy, vibrant, alive. Once I even felt brilliant. But I think I had just had a pomegranate martini.

I've been with people I shouldn't have and I've walked away from more than one good man. I have longed for a relationship and I have treasured my singledom.

And through all of the changes of these past few years, I have enjoyed dating. And that's what I want to share with you. I date a lot. Well, if you consider eighty-seven dates in two years a lot. And that's just an approximation.

Of course, there were times that I didn't date at all. Sometimes I felt too tired, too busy, too fat. And sometimes I felt lonely. Lost. Low.

But I know that low doesn't have to be my final destination. Getting down is fine; being under is okay, too; but low is banished. I'm going for back on top. Come with me. I know you'll like the view from there.

Chapter 2

It's Just Dating

THE MAIN THING I WANT TO TELL YOU ABOUT DATING IS that it is *just dating*. And I would encourage you—hell, I'd like to inspire you—to simply *date*.

It's not dating-to-find-my-next-boyfriend. Dating-to-avoid-being-alone. Dating-to-complete-myself. And God forbid, it's not dating-to-get-married. You don't have to date for security or to meet some societal standard of couplehood. On the other hand, you don't have to date just because I'm suggesting it, just because your aunt wants to fix you up, or just because some guy asked you out—you will end up dating a lot of assholes that way. Well, no matter what you do, you may wind up dating a few assholes.

But that's okay. Like I said, it's just dating.

And I think if we put it in perspective and slip our sense of humor into our purse right next to our lipstick, dating can be a lot of fun. But it may not be fun *all* the time, and it certainly will not cure all of life's problems.

Solo Does Not Mean Lonely

While it might sound contrary to the message of this book, I'm suggesting you also spend a little time alone after your divorce.

On the nights when your ex has the dog or the kids (if you have a dog or a kid), or your neighborhood is having a couples dinner party, or you finished work early, don't feel as if you have to have a date. Do something else you enjoy—go to the bookstore, work out, meet a girlfriend for dinner, shop, see a movie, or just hang out in your own home, solo.

I love being in my house by myself, and I never thought I'd say that. I clean a little, work a little, organize closets a little (actually, I do this a lot). It's quiet. It's nice. And I am really fine that no one is there whispering those three little words: *What's for dinner?*

There's also no one rushing me or asking me to do something for them. Instead, alone in my house, it's amazingly peaceful.

Before my divorce, I thought all I would do is cry the entire time that my son was with his dad. Okay, I did cry a little. But you learn to cherish your alone time. And you know what? If you and your ex can keep things civil and friendly, then you realize your child(ren) and their father have an incredible thing going, too. Your ex can do things *his* way with your kids, without you asking him to do it your way—without you asking him to do anything at all. They'll manage. They'll survive. In fact, they'll *thrive*. I have a few friends whose parents divorced when they were kids and they tell me it was great to have another house to go to when things got stressful with one parent.

> **Alone in my house, it's amazingly peaceful.**

I think one of the reasons I could not imagine being divorced is that I could not picture my son—my baby, my toddler, my kindergartner—without me for a weekend. I couldn't imagine *me* without *him,* either. Sometimes I think I gave all my love to my son when my marriage wasn't working out. Can you imagine how heavy that must have been for him? Can you imagine if it went on like that throughout his entire childhood? His adolescence? I mean today, at eleven, he is embarrassed by my mere existence. He only hugs me or says *I love you* in the privacy of our own home. I'm okay with that.

The point is, I'm happier now, my ex is happier *and* healthier now, and quite frankly I think my son is reaping the benefits.

So try to enjoy your alone time. Spend it wisely or foolishly— it doesn't matter. It's your time. If you want to date, great. If not, don't. When you're ready, *if* you're ready, you'll do it. After all, there will always be forty million single men online.

When my ex-college-boyfriend told me about his post-divorce dating experience, he said, "Even when you think you're ready to date, you're probably still a year away from *really* being ready." I think his advice was dead-on, and I've heard it many times since.

My First Date . . . Again

My first date after thirteen years of marriage was incredibly awkward, and I really thought I was ready. I was so *not.*

In fact, I seriously thought it might be another thirteen years before I'd do it again.

> I really thought I was ready. I was so *not.*

On the bright side, my first date was intelligent, nice looking, and possessed one of my favorite must-haves: a sense of humor. This was especially impressive because he is a doctor. Correction: a *surgeon.*

I think I should have started with a paperboy.

On my drive home from the date that night, I replayed in my mind every excruciating moment—and I had a feeling I'd broken every dating rule ever written. So when I arrived home, I Googled "dating don'ts." Sure enough, I had unwittingly committed nearly every one. The only thing missing was my photo, hanging above the list like a Wild West wanted poster. In the sixty-watt clarity of my desk lamp, each of the rules seemed so obvious:

- **Do not talk about your ex-spouse on a first date.** Not only did I talk about my ex, I practically told his entire life story, starting from conception: his terrible childhood, his resultant baggage, his brilliant mind, and the fact that, although he is my ex, we're still good friends and I love him. At this point, I'm sure my date was trying to figure out how long it would be before my ex and I were back together . . . unless he was too busy looking for the restaurant's emergency exit. Thankfully, I left out the part about my ex having intimacy issues and all that that implies. How I managed to contain this part of the story, I have no idea. I must have actually let my date speak. Or, perhaps seeing where I was going with this story line, he was kind enough to interrupt me.

- **Do not mention sex on a first date.** Well, technically, I did not break this rule, as I believe this actually means you're not supposed to mention that you'd like to *have* sex. But here's what happened. I was telling my date that one of my jobs involves researching and writing about teens and their issues. When my date asked what the research showed, I could have mentioned peer pressure, drinking and driving, cyberbullying. But no, I had the uncommon good sense to talk about the recent trend of girls giving boys oral sex as routinely as those of us from decades past used to French-kiss. Only I didn't say "oral sex," I said "blow jobs." Talk about polite dinner conversation! According to my Google search, this is grounds for an immediate end to any date, unless you're actually *offering* said blow job. To be fair, my date did not seem put off and, in fact, said he had heard about this trend. Still, I don't think I scored any extra points in the ladylike department when I tried backpedaling, "Don't get me wrong, I'm all for oral sex." What in the world was he supposed to make of that? Although he did seem to perk up a bit.

- **Do not mention your date's ex on a first date.** I don't know how we got on this one, but in fact, both of my date's exes were mentioned. Unlike me, he was smart enough to give abbreviated versions. At least I was able to rein in my journalistic tendency to ask ten questions in sixty seconds. One point for me. Not nearly enough to make up for my failing score.

- **Ladies should not drink beer on a first date.** Not only did I order and drink a beer, I explained to my date that the cafe we were patronizing used to carry a fabulous beer that was no longer available due to the fact that the brewery—which had been owned by a woman—was recently shut down and I was terribly disappointed because it was one of the best-tasting beers I had ever had and if I could I would buy that brewery. Yes, I actually said that, and without a breath, just like it reads here. At which point my date said, naturally, "Oh, you really know your beers." I don't think he meant it as a compliment.

- **Do not talk about marriage on a first date.** Now, to my credit, I didn't start this topic of conversation. My date asked me what I thought made for a good marriage. I have no idea why he asked me, since I had already made it clear that I had recently come to the conclusion that marriage pretty much kills a relationship. In fact, I said that I supported Katharine Hepburn's view of marriage and quoted her as saying "Married couples should live near each other and visit frequently." (By the way, there is no rule about trashing marriage on a first date; I think the rule-writers felt that this was so obvious, it need not be mentioned. Obviously, they were wrong.) In hindsight, I think the question about what makes a good marriage is one of those Miss America–type questions, where I should have given a non-answer answer about saving the world and feeding the hungry. Instead, coming from the marriage I was in (see above), the first thing I said was "Sexual compatibility." My date tried to help me out, saying that surely I meant the greater good of intimacy and closeness. I guess that was *his* Miss America response. But I was steadfast in my answer. After a while, my senses returned and I remembered to mention honesty, trust, respect, friendship, and the true number one for me, sense of humor. So maybe he thought I was kidding all along. One can only hope.

> **Maybe he thought I was kidding all along. One can only hope.**

- **Do not reveal your shortcomings on a first date.** Does this even need to be said? Apparently to me it does. Of course, it goes without saying that I broke this rule unintentionally, but toward the end of the evening it became painfully apparent that I had learned geography from the high school football coach, and that I am still geographically challenged. In fact, I can sum up my entire first date in a single word: *Okinawa.* You see, my date was very well traveled, and we spoke about the places he'd been, the things he'd seen, and a few of the countries we had both been to. At one point it suddenly got noisy in the cafe—it must have thrown me, because up until that point we had been the only people in the place. Right about then my date said that one of his favorite journeys took him to "Nawa." That's all I heard: "Nawa." It sounded Hawaiian or Japanese, but

I couldn't be sure of what he'd said, so I asked, "Where?" *If only I had asked, "What?"* (Do you see the subtle difference?) And he said, drily, "Okinawa. You know, Pearl Harbor?" Which I translated to mean: "You actually graduated college?" I nodded with what I hoped was a knowledgeable look, but my head was swimming: Geography *and* world history in the same sentence? (I was taught world history by the high school *basketball* coach.) By now, the notion of excusing myself to go to the ladies' room and crawling out the window was looking like my best bet. As a footnote, I did Google "Pearl Harbor" and "Okinawa" later that night. I guess the connection is that the attack on Pearl Harbor brought the United States into the war and Okinawa was the last major battle of the war. But I swear I think my date said Pearl Harbor was *in* Okinawa. So now I'm wondering if he's slapping himself on the head going, "How dumb am I? Did I actually say Pearl Harbor is in Okinawa?" Maybe we both sum up our date with that one word . . .

• **Do not kiss good night on the first date.** *Gotcha.* You don't actually think I got close to breaking this rule, do you? Instead, I did the awkward shaking hands with my non-hand-shaking-hand thing. It was like I was possessed by my grandmother. And then, as if straight out of *The Mary Tyler Moore Show,* I said I'd be glad to help if he ever needed information about things to do or see in Atlanta. I didn't offer to take him or go with him, just to point him in the right direction. After that, *I* wouldn't even ask me out on a second date, and I *know* all the really good stuff about me. Needless to say, there was no "I hope to see you again" or "call me sometime." It wasn't until I got into my car that I realized I hadn't taken a breath for the past three hours. Surely the lack of oxygen was responsible for my impossibly geeky behavior, right? If I had only passed out, the evening would have gone much better.

I actually found twenty-two "don'ts" on my Google search. Among the ones I managed to avoid were:

- **Don't smoke.** Not cigarettes, not marijuana, not crack cocaine.

- **Do not bring your child.** *Duh.* I also left the baby album in the car at the last minute. So there.

- **Do not wear a low-cut or revealing top.** In hindsight, this might have helped things considerably.

- **Do not recite from the Bible.** Although I managed to steer clear of both testaments, I did quote a *People* magazine article, which is actually number eleven on the "don'ts" list.

- **Do not tell your parents you are going on a date,** especially when it is with a doctor-correction-surgeon. (Actually, I didn't manage to avoid this rule.) When I called my folks the next day to give them a very brief synopsis, I heard my father yell to my mother, "Cancel the caterer, honey." I then explained that I wouldn't be telling them about any future dates since I never again wanted to make that day-after-the-date phone call. For this, my mother did not speak to me for two weeks—which was actually the silver lining to this whole ordeal.

So while I didn't have a great rate-a-date score, I'm still glad I went out. It's just dating, remember? Of course, I'll never do a three-hour first date again. Stick with coffee. A drink. A pre-arranged exit strategy.

I'm hoping there will be a lot of dating in your future, but there is only one first date after your divorce. I'm lucky mine was with a nice guy. He walked me to my car, and even made a thoughtful, understanding comment about the necessities of motherhood when I pointed out that mine was the minivan among the BMWs and Lex-uses (Lex-i?). I had considered renting a convertible for the evening but nixed the idea when I thought about how strange it would be if we made it to date number two and I had to explain why my cool car had turned into a mommy-mobile. Obviously, I

> There will be a lot of dating in your future, but there is only one first date after your divorce.

needn't have concerned myself about the possibility of date number two. (By the way, showing up in that minivan? That was on the list, too—violation of rule number twenty-two.)

When you do decide to date again (if, after reading about my first date, you *do* decide to date again), I hope you will take pleasure in the act of dating itself. Enjoy meeting new people, hearing new stories, learning what other people know and like and do. But go on a date because you *choose* to, because you *want* to—not because you think you are obligated in any way or you are afraid of being alone.

With your cats.

And a box of Krispy Kreme donuts.

Watching *Law & Order* reruns.

Okay, maybe we *should* check out the guy your aunt wants to fix you up with . . .

Chapter 3

The Truth about Divorce Rates

I WAS ONE OF THOSE PEOPLE WHO THOUGHT I'D BE MARRIED forever. After all, my parents have been married for fifty-one years (to each other), and my sister and brothers have each been married almost thirty years (*not* to each other). That means I have about 150 years of marriage in my immediate family alone.

It just never occurred to me that my husband and I wouldn't make it. On the other hand, I have several girlfriends who tell me they knew their marriage wouldn't last—they knew it even as they were walking down the aisle. You may have been one of those brides hyperventilating into her bouquet. I definitely understand this, I'm just saying that the possibility of divorce was not what I was thinking about as I said my vows in front of a hundred of my parents' closest friends and the twenty that I was allowed to invite. I was thinking, *This is my dream. This is my future. I'm sure I can change him.*

Numbers Lie

Even though I was well aware of the statistical evidence that more than 50 percent of all marriages don't last, I just didn't think I would end up in that half. Like I said, I never had any divorce role models. And anyway, I have my own theories on the so-called divorce rates:

First, any woman who marries a jerk and divorces him, it shouldn't count. He's a jerk. You get out of jail free. Doesn't count.

Second, anyone who gets divorced and remarries her ex-spouse and then divorces him again—that should only count once. Hello? Elizabeth Taylor and Richard Burton were rich, famous, and beautiful and they couldn't make it work the first *or* second time. How about Melanie Griffith and Don Johnson? Or Richard Pryor? He remarried two of his exes—that's four divorces. (Although to quote the fabulously funny TMZ .com staff on Pryor, "When you're freebasing a kilo of coke a day, it doesn't matter who your wife is as long as she knows CPR.") All by themselves these few celebrities raised the divorce rate, like, 8 percent. Remarrying and redivorcing an ex-spouse is like bad déjà vu. It should only count once.

> **Any woman who marries a jerk and divorces him, it shouldn't count.**

And speaking of celebrities, I don't think that their divorces should be tallied into the divorce rates with us regular folk anyway. While I may talk about Jen and Brad and Angelina and Uma and Ethan as if we are all friends, they are *not* real people who make the same kinds of mistakes as we do. I know it hurts when they break up all over the front pages, but when they fall in love on the set of a romantic comedy or on an island somewhere and then they go back to their real lives and real property and real paparazzi and real nannies, all similarities to my life end, and I will not have their divorces escalating the rates for everyone else. Period.

This is why I didn't put a lot of weight into the fact that 50 percent of all marriages end in divorce. Marrying jerks? Remarrying jerks? Inter-actor marriages? No wonder the number is so high. In my little corner of the world, everyone stayed married till death did them part. I was young and in love and getting married (and I did not write in my wedding notice that *this is the first marriage for both the bride and groom*). If all of us thought we'd be one of those wives with only a fifty–fifty chance of making it, would we really go through with it? The years of dating, the waiting for the proposal, the dreaming of the ring, the cajoling over the wedding details, the endless registering for stuff no one gives you anyway, the selection of the ridiculously priced dress that you will only wear once (no matter how many times you get married), and the dieting to fit into the ridiculously priced dress. Would you do it if you were destined to divorce? I don't think so.

My Own Personal Divorce Denial

Here's how much in denial I was: I made an *America's Funniest Home Videos* parody for my rehearsal dinner, filled with jokes about how I knew I could make love last and why the divorce rates didn't bother me. I was blatantly smug about overcoming such concerns as incompatible lifestyles (slob versus obsessively neat), living with a musician (and on a musician's income), and keeping the fires burning. What the hell did I know? I had only been dating my soon-to-be-husband for four months before he proposed, and I'd only been engaged for six!

When I watch that video, it's painful to see that blissfully ignorant girl—that pre-divorced version of myself—poking fun at what would become serious issues that threatened the status of my new-wife self-confidence. There I am, captured for all eternity on VHS (until we transfer it to DVD), wearing a blond wig over my natural red hair, snapping a costume-store whip and sporting a scuba mask and saying all kinds of snarky things about making love last—words that only a soon-to-be-bride in complete denial could possibly say before she's ever been married. It was just a two-minute video. But what I didn't know then would take a feature film to explore.

And I am talking *serious* denial. I mean, my ex and I were in couples therapy for our entire engagement. Most people would have seen that as some sort of sign, or at least it would have given them pause. Not me. After waiting my whole life for a real marriage proposal—my mother and me both, actually—nothing as trivial as a little childhood baggage could stop us. Just four months after we met, my ex proposed to me on a Sunday morning; we told my parents around noon, and by six o'clock that evening my mother had a date, a room, a band, a caterer. The train had left the station, ladies and gentleman, and I was strapped to it.

> What I didn't know then would take a feature film to explore.

To be fair, even if someone had told me that maybe I should slow things down, I don't think I would have listened. I still believed that love conquers all—that my own personal brand of love could fix whatever was wrong with the man I adored.

That was, of course, the first lesson I learned and the first tip I will pass on to you:

Tip 1: Love does not cure all. In fact, you shouldn't even be thinking about curing or fixing or changing the person whom you're dating. You should instead be seeking someone who already works really well all by himself, as well as with who you are and what you want.

Now, I don't know much about what makes a good marriage. I don't even know much about what makes a good divorce. But I do know that the majority of men I talk to, and at least half of the women, would like to someday be in a satisfying relationship that makes them happy, not crazy.

The first step, of course, is to believe that post-divorce dating doesn't suck. Sure, every date won't be great—but really, what is consistently great every time except maybe a Hershey's Kiss?

So here are the rest of my first post-divorce dating tips:

Tip 2: When you think you are ready to date, you probably aren't. In fact, you probably won't really be ready for another year. As long as you know you're not ready and you go easy on yourself (and the dates), you'll be fine. It's like a dress rehearsal.

Tip 3: Try for a nice divorce. (Those of you who married the jerks, I know this is asking a lot. But try.) This will make it so much easier when your date asks why you got divorced. If you and your ex are on good terms, you will more likely avoid calling all men assholes when discussing your ex. This is a good thing, especially on a first date.

Tip 4: Never, ever think you must date. I don't care how many times you say "Not yet" when married friends who think they are just being supportive ask if you are dating. Unless they offer you the name, age, photo, and financial and mental health records of an eligible bachelor, simply ask them if they are still having oral sex. I think this is equally polite dinner conversation, don't you? If you are out there dating because you think that you should or that this is your one last chance, dating really will suck.

Tip 5: Never let a first date pick you up at your home. In fact, I would wait until half a dozen dates and a clean NetDetective.com search before you let him pick you up at all. Then I would wait another six months until he picks you up when your child(ren) is home. Your kids absolutely do not need to be involved in any of your new friendships. It can make them scared, angry, hopeful, or any number of emotions that have nothing to do with your dating reality. (See chapter 17.)

Tip 6: Meet in a place that is convenient to you. Pick a place that you frequent often. Make friends with the management and bartenders. You'll feel comfortable meeting dates here—and you may be coming here a lot. However (and I learned this the hard way), if you tend to show any PDA (public display of affection), choose a place outside your neighborhood. You never know whose friend of a friend will be watching.

One Sunday morning I got a call from one of my oldest friends.

"Were you at Via's last night?" she asked.

"Yes, I had a dinner date," I said.

"Yeah, I know. Margie was there and she said you two were all but horizontal."

Long pause. All. But. Horizontal. You gotta be kidding me. I felt myself blush—not because I was embarrassed (not really, anyway) but because I was pissed. Particularly because other than a nice (okay, really nice) good night kiss and some huddling in the rain while we waited for our cars, we were pretty hands-off. At least in my book.

But nobody wants to hear about an innocent little kiss; everyone wants to hear the *Sex and the City* adaptation. And why are a bunch of couples (most of whom I don't even know) talking about my date and me in the first place? Is this the dinner-conversation version of married foreplay? And did I used to do that, too?

Tip 7: Do not make a first date for dinner, or for anything lasting longer than one hour. Tell your date that you have some time in between meetings or car pools or whatever, and you'd love to grab coffee or a drink. My friend Bonnie—who has so many dates each week we say she's "power dating"—is the one who taught me this rule. Unless it's fabulous, get in and get out in less than an hour. In fact, her dates are so short she calls them "encounters"—as in, "I had three Match .com encounters this week."

So, before your date starts, set your cell phone alarm to ring in one hour. Or have a friend call you. Be prepared to give that friend an excuse for missing your appointment if you are having a good time, or talk to her as if she's on her deathbed if you're not. My own advice that I don't always take? Leave him wanting more; don't stay longer than an hour (two, max). You're busy!

> Unless it's fabulous, get in and get out in less than an hour.

Tip 8: Don't do anything too stupid. This is my one consistent rule that I recommend for nearly everything in life. I also have dozens of "stupid Ginger stories" so obviously it doesn't always stick.

Chapter 4
Making Your Manfile

DO WE NEED TO UNDERSTAND WHY WE MARRIED OUR EX and why we divorced him in order to know how to date afterward? Because that could take approximately . . . *forfrickin'ever.* Every woman I spoke with said we need to at least look at what we liked and didn't like, what we were willing to put up with and what we weren't. You don't have to overanalyze it or interview your ex or take a poll among your friends (like I did); you just need a clue about what you were attracted to and what you couldn't stand anymore so you can use this information as the basis for creating your Manfile. That's right, your *Manfile:* a list of characteristics and qualities you will not put up with in the next guy you choose. It's also a list of what you *will* seek—make that *require*—in anyone who wants to get close to you.

I think it makes sense to start with your most recent past and work backward.

Step 1: Write down all the things you didn't like about your latest ex—things you really hated as well as things that simply annoyed the hell out of you.

Step 2: Write down anything you didn't like about *all* of your previous exes. What were the deal-breakers with past boyfriends, husbands, or dates? Now you have the beginnings of your non-negotiables. Non-negotiables are just one part of the Manfile. They are the things about which you will not compromise; the characteristics that, if a guy possesses them, you will not be sucked into a relationship with him.

Step 3: Write down your answer to this question: *What did you learn about* yourself *from the things you hated about your exes?* This is important, because it will show you qualities about yourself that you may want to work on before your next relationship. For example, I hated the fact that my ex did not take care of himself—he didn't eat right, didn't exercise, didn't take his prescribed medications correctly. It pissed me off. Over the years I've learned that my anger was really based on my fear: fear that he would die young, leave our son without a dad, leave me without a partner.

Is "taking care of yourself" still a non-negotiable for me? Yes. But it's no longer because I'm afraid of being "left." It's because I enjoy being active, fit, and healthy, and whoever wants to be with me will have to like those things, too (and drag my ass to the gym when I'm feeling particularly unmotivated). I also have no desire to "save" someone (finally!), so if a guy doesn't take care of himself, I'm not attracted to him.

Now that you've taken a look at yourself, let's get back to him. A few of my girlfriends and I have worked on our non-negotiables, and here are some of the things we wrote down that we will never accept: lying; abuse (physical, verbal, substance, alcohol); arrogance; cheating; a guy who is judgmental; violent;

self-destructive; mean; impatient; financially unstable; manipulative; sloppy; boring.

I know some of these are more serious offenses than others, but don't worry about it. This is your list, your boundaries, your non-negotiables. No one else has to see it, agree with it, or be beholden to it. Hell, you don't even have to hold yourself accountable to it. But by putting this list down on paper, you help define what you are looking for, and what you are not.

Step 4: The next leg of your Manfile is the list of qualities that you *do* want in a partner. I call these your *must-haves*. Yes, it involves making another list. (C'mon, it's not like a big art project. Just sharpen your pencil, okay?) What are the things you've loved about other relationships that you absolutely must have again? What are the things you *haven't* had in a relationship that caused you to dump it? What must the next guy in your life have in order for you to consider a long-term relationship with him?

> By putting this list down on paper, you help define what you are looking for, and what you are not.

Looking over my girlfriends' lists, here are our top must-haves: honesty; sense of humor; financial stability; intelligence; sexual compatibility/intimacy; mental health; respect; kindness; physical fitness; a willingness to grow; flexibility. There are, of course, variations on these characteristics. Feel free to write "hot" instead of fit; "wealth" instead of financial stability; "brilliance" instead of intelligence.

You might require qualities such as successful (or at least currently employed), spiritual or religious, loves kids/dogs/hamsters—whatever you want gets to go on the list because it's *your* must-haves!

Step 5: The final part of your Manfile is your nice-to-haves—sort of an expansive wish list. Get as detailed as you want, because I imagine this to be the blueprint that the world consults when it fixes you up. Nice-to-haves could include height, weight, income, family situation (such as has a big family or has no kids), career, location; it could include specifics such as plays volleyball, owns a lake house, loves redheads (that's on my list), balances work/life, has his own friends, has great abs, is outgoing, loves giving foot massages . . . hey, this is your nice-to-haves, make 'em good!

Word of caution: I believe in the power of these lists. I believe that when you commit them to paper, you begin to draw that person into your life. So be very clear and aware and inclusive about what you write. Then get ready. The first time I wrote my list was in 1987, two years before I met my ex-husband. I did not know then the power of a Manfile. I had things on that list that are still on my list today—honesty, sense of humor, intelligence—but being in my early twenties, I also had things like musician, ponytail, earring (this is slightly embarrassing, but it's true). When my husband showed up in my life, he was indeed a ponytailed, one-earringed musician who was brilliant and very funny. Looking back, I wish I had put in some other stuff, but I was in my twenties, who knew you had to ask for sex? You're laughing, aren't you? It's okay. I've laughed about it, too. That's why I'm really, really careful about what I write, when I write it, and when I declare that the list is finished (never). There's always something else I think of. And one more caution: Be careful what you wish for.

Now that you are armed with your Manfile, tuck it away in your purse or wallet and read it often. You'll probably add to it from time to time; you may even delete something that is no longer a non-negotiable for you. Unfortunately, I can't promise that it will keep you from making bad choices once in a while—a one-night stand with a visiting Cirque du Soleil performer, or a doomed-from-the-start romance with a sexy bad boy . . . you really have to be your own best friend here. But it will help you remember not to compromise on those things that you won't put up with, as well as those things that you must have in a relationship, or you'll wind up right back here, instead of back on top.

> **One more caution: Be careful what you wish for.**

Chapter 5

Today's Dating Means Putting Your Life Online

THE MOST FREQUENT QUESTION DIVORCED WOMEN ASK ME is: "Can you believe what my ex-husband did this time?" But that's not what this book is about. So the second most frequent question divorced women ask me is: "Where can I find quality men?" I love that they don't say *a quality man;* the women I talk to want options. And I believe it is—at least in part—a numbers game. The more men you meet, the more likely you are to find someone who has the qualities you want in a partner, whether it's short-term, long-term, or just to impress your friends at your twentieth high school reunion.

I have talked to men and women of all ages, and most of them tell me they don't consider the bar scene a good spot for finding their next true partner. It's loud, it's crowded, and there's sticky stuff all over the floor. It's not conducive to great conversation, and whatever pearls of wisdom and wit do occur are often blurred by strong martinis or several glasses of wine (or both). In all my years of dating, I have perhaps met three men at bars whom I actually dated (not all in one night, of course). This is like 0.00003 percent. Not great odds.

Online Dating Grows Up

So unless you've been living on an island for the past decade (one without WiFi, or a Starbucks for that matter), you know that one of the most prolific ways to meet people is through online dating sites. What you may not know is that men and women of all sizes, looks, ages, IQs, incomes, backgrounds, and ethnicities are on these sites. Online dating is no longer viewed as desperate, corny, or sleazy; it's not "one day we'll laugh about the way we met" anymore. It's a microcosm of the world we actually live in—everything from hottie to nottie, from newly divorced to never been married, from Wall Street to ex-con (sometimes in the same guy).

There are sites for singles, swingers, spirituals, seniors, fitness junkies, ex-junkies, women-seeking-Christians, Christians-seeking-Jews. There are sites dedicated to Asian singles, Indian singles, international singles, African American singles, and sites dedicated to bringing them all together. There are sites for girls who want to date girls, men who want to *be* girls, guys who want to *dress* like girls. Sites for gay men, gay women, and those who are bi-curious. I'm telling you, no matter what you are looking for in the name of love, there's an online dating service waiting to serve you. The one you choose will depend on where you are in your dating life cycle, what you want in a relationship (*if* you want

> No matter what you are looking for in the name of love, there's an online dating service waiting to serve you.

a relationship), and how far to the left or right you're willing to swing.

That said, I have to admit that I am still surprised when I meet a good-looking twenty-something who is on a dating site. I mean, if you're not clubbing in your twenties, what are you doing? But one young, good-looking waiter in South Beach gave me a great answer when I learned he was on Match.com and I asked him why. He said when you go to a bar, you don't know anything about the women you meet there except that they wound up at that particular bar on that particular night. When you meet someone from an online dating site, though, you see what they look like, you know a little about their story, their likes and dislikes, what you have in common, how old they are, where they're from, and you've had a chance to talk with them—by e-mail, IM, or phone—before you ever go out. This particular waiter said he loves online dating because it gives him so much more information about so many girls in such a relatively short amount of time.

And he's not out fifty bucks in drink tabs.

You Have to Pay to Play

Still, online dating does take time and a learn-as-you-go mind-set. And most sites have a monthly fee ranging from $9.99 to $45.99, depending on the plan you choose. (There are notable exceptions, including Craigslist and Plenty of Fish, or POF as it's known to singles all over the world. Sites like these are free.) Typically, though, you have to pay to play. But seriously, when don't you?

I think it's money well spent, because online dating is the place where you will find the most men per minute. In fact, I don't see a better venue for women over forty. It's not as if we're going to hang out at bars and clubs. Well, not all the time anyway. With millions of guys on the sites, the odds of discovering a few strong candidates are pretty good. In fact, maybe the next presidential election should be run like an online dating site—the candidates fill out an online profile, post their favorite pictures, describe themselves in two paragraphs or less, list their turn-ons, turn-offs, and political leanings, and the one with the most clicks wins.

> **Online dating is the place where you will find the most men per minute.**

But we're talking about finding dates, not running the country, so of the most popular sites out there— eHarmony, Match.com, Lavalife, Yahoo! Personals, Chemistry. com, TRUE.com, FriendFinder, Perfectmatch, Fitness Singles, Friendster, Craigslist—how do you know which one is right for you?

Finding the Right Site

Well, when I decided to try virtual dating, I found that the dating sites range from those that promise to "find your soulmate in three easy steps and 436 multiple-choice questions" to "find someone who wants to have sex with you tonight in any city in the United States and Thailand."

I certainly wasn't ready for the forever-thing, but I didn't want to have gratuitous sex, either (well, not *just* gratuitous sex). And I couldn't imagine anyone was actually looking for that from a midforties, self-employed, suburban single mom, unless that's some sort of fetish, which, after exploring the Web sites at the far end of the dating spectrum, I'm sure there must be a **chat*** group for.

The first site I signed up for was the middle-of-the-road, Dr.-Phil-spokespersoned Match.com. As an aside, you'd be surprised by how many people on Match are also on those far-end-of-the-spectrum sites.

As I found myself cyberstrolling through the **profiles** of SMs (Single Males), SBMs (Single Black Males), DJMs (Divorced Jewish Males)—(stopping at every picture featuring a shirtless guy whose profile said, "Sorry, this was the only picture I had" . . . uh-*huh*)—I realized that most of the people I met online were as clueless as I was about e-etiquette, the tools of the trade, online lingo, and those unending variations on the smiley face—**emoticons.** ;)

So I checked out a few other sites, too. Okay, *quite* a few. During the past two years, I've been on seven dating sites, and I've been registered on as many as four at a time. This leads me to my first online dating tip:

*This term and others that you might not be familiar with are explained in the sidebar on page 76.

Tip 1: I recommend no more than two sites at a time. The reason? You start to get addicted to checking your inboxes a dozen times a day to find out who's **viewing** you, who's **flirting** with you, who's sending you an e-mail, and who's replying to your e-mails. I am not kidding, this may be the most hazardous part of online dating—the amount of time you spend **IMing** and chatting and clicking, in front of your computer, late at night, and sometimes when you should be working.

Tip 2: Definitely do not take your new friends to work with you, especially if you work for someone else. Many workplaces monitor your e-mails and IMs, which means not only is your company saving your entire online history to some internal server, but the trail also shows how much time you're spending on extra-curricular activities when you should be getting out that TPS report. When I first started talking to people online, my workday stretched from ten hours to fourteen, easily. Plus, you have no idea when a casual IM conversation will take a turn into a more erogenous zone, and that will likely be just the time when your boss walks up behind you and your computer screen to introduce you to the new corporate owners.

Even after I weaned myself from my inbox addiction, my own personal stats look as if I couldn't possibly have done anything productive (other than date online) for the past two years. But actually, these numbers are probably pretty typical, or even on the low side:

I have received 6,000 e-mails; my profile has been viewed more than 38,177 times (and no, not all by the same guy); I have

IM'd and chatted with more than 100 people; I have 22 actual friends on my instant message list; I have been on dates with 39 guys I met online; and I have had four long-term friendships or relationships that started with a single online "hello."

Now you know why people tell you they don't have time to date online—it's like having a second career. But think how many hours you would (you do?) spend *offline* looking for love in bookstores, Starbucks, health clubs, sporting events, grocery stores, friends' parties, singles parties, airports, and bars chatting and positioning and trying to find just one guy you'd like to have a conversation with. Plus, in case you've forgotten, having a relationship takes time, too, so let's just consider the online hours a warm-up to tone your stamina and build your endurance. You're going to need it for the next tip:

> My profile has been viewed more than 38,177 times (and no, not all by the same guy).

Tip 3: I recommend that you stay active on a site for at least six months. It can easily take that long to search, sift, and schedule a single solid prospect. However, I also recommend a get-in-and-get-out approach. I'm the poster child for getting to know someone online as an initial step, but if, after ten back-and-forth e-mails trying to find a day and time to meet in the non-virtual world, your online prospect can't commit, I say it's not worth it. Either he's not serious about meeting you or he *is* serious—with someone else—and is keeping you on the line as a just-in-case option. I've been there and it's crazy frustrating. Of course, it took me a while to figure this out—I'd be e-mailing with a guy trying to sync our schedules to meet for a first date when I'd finally realize we'd been trying for more than a month and couldn't get the stars to align for even a drink. This is a sign from above: Move on.

That's why my favorite sites are those that let you get on quickly and get a look around. Match.com, Fitness-Singles.com, Lavalife, Craigslist—you don't have to fill out lengthy questionnaires, get a background check, insert your credit card information, or go in for psychological counseling. You just type "female," "divorced," and your zip code and you're on. Then you can browse around and see if the site is worth joining. (Most sites offer a free trial period.)

On the other hand (this would be the left hand), if you are serious about finding a serious relationship, eHarmony, Catholic-Match, and other more marriage-focused matchmaking sites may be worth the extra time. Some of these sites will actually put your information through a kind of techno Dr. Ruth and send *you* the profiles of men they think are compatible with you, based on your answers. eHarmony founder Neil Clark Warren bases his online matchmaking on twenty-nine compatibility areas. I didn't even know there *were* twenty-nine compatibility areas. So, while you have to put in eHarmony time upfront, you may actually save search time on the back end. And we all like a smaller back end. That is, of course, if you trust someone else to find you a match. A lot of people dislike eHarmony for the very reason others love it—it takes work, commitment, and patience. And sometimes the system still doesn't come up with a guy you'd want to have lunch with, much less date. But several of my friends are dating eHarmony guys, so I would say it's a matter of preference and what you are looking for.

My ex is the only person I've ever heard of who, after completing the lengthy eHarmony form, was sent a reply that said something to the effect of, "While we have millions of single female members, the total number of compatible matches we found for you totals: 0. Good luck in your continued search for love."

I'm not sure if it was his occupation (musician) or his income (he likes to select the lowest range) or his religious affiliation (ardent agnostic). Come to think of it, he never was very good at multiple-choice questions.

My ex's experience aside, I actually do believe that there *is* a site for everyone. Online daters fall into four main categories, and it's helpful to see where you might land:

- Looking for a long-term relationship (LTR).

- Looking for a casual relationship.

- Looking to get married. (Please see chapter 2 about dating with this goal in mind.)

- Just looking to get laid.

Of course, there are a lot of options within each of these categories. For example, if you are looking for an LTR and being with someone of the same religion is a non-negotiable for you, then I recommend starting with a faith-based singles site such as Christian Cafe, CatholicMatch, BigChurch, or JDate. And while these sites aren't completely xenophobic and certainly no one's ever tried to convert me, you might want to think through the whole religion requirement from your post-divorced-dating perspective. Years of Yeshiva or parochial school aside, your feelings on the topic of religion and other previous must-haves may have changed.

Before I was married, being with someone who practiced the same religion I did seemed important. After all, I thought marriage would be complicated enough without having to merge Christmas and Chanukah, brises and baptisms, confirmations and consecrations. Plus, all I know about Jesus Christ I learned from a Broadway musical.

But after your divorce, some of that may not matter as much to you. If you have kids, you are probably already raising them in the faith you've selected—no matter who you date next. And I, for one, am hoping not to deal with in-laws or their opinions on religion. Let's say you're not even planning to get married anytime soon—would you consider dating someone outside of your religion, ethnicity, or age range?

Tip 4: When you're making your Manfile (see chapter 4), **think about what really matters to you in a partner, and what might simply be old thought patterns or societal pressures.** You certainly expand the playing field if you broaden your options, but don't compromise on anything that is important to you. That's why you create a list of non-negotiables in the first place. Just write them in pencil, in case you change your mind.

My first faith-based site was JDate.com. It's for Jewish singles, whether they've ever been married or not. While odds are that your date will be a Member of the Tribe, you don't have to be Jewish to join. I don't think you even have to be circumcised.

Are You Going to Eat That?

I was on JDate for more than a year and I had several dates. The first man I went out with was about ten years older than I was. You don't know this about me yet, but this is an anomaly for me. I tend to skew toward much younger men (that's *skew*). Still, I went.

Right away I could tell that Saul was southern Jewish, which is different from any other kind of Jewish. It's a combination of extreme politeness (drawl and all) with an undercurrent of irrational inferiority complex. Saul's kids were grown, he had been a member of our city's close-knit Jewish community for a long time, and it appeared that he didn't get out much.

We met for bagels (cliché, I know), and as soon as we started talking I realized this was a mistake. My best friend told me later that she could have predicted this outcome, but as you *do* know by now, I don't always listen. So here I am, an independent, extroverted, wisecracking, ultra-Reform Jewish redhead whom no one in their right-leaning mind would ever tag as "conservative," breaking bread with a traditional, old-school southern Jewish man. Put your money on the table, we're taking all bets.

Because it was December, Saul and I were talking about the upcoming holidays. I mentioned that I had a few parties to attend the next weekend. Saul says, "You're going to holiday parties this weekend? Isn't it true they're really Christmas parties? Isn't that what you mean?"

I felt like I was being cross-examined by a Yiddish Perry Mason.

I thought for a moment, not understanding why he was making the distinction. "Uh, yes, well, I guess they are mostly Christmas parties," I said. "Most of them are being thrown by friends of mine who celebrate Christmas."

"Well," he says, taking a giant bite of his Everything bagel, "Goys do love free food."

I am not kidding. This is a direct quote.

For those of you who do not know, *Goy* is a Yiddish synonym for Gentile or non-Jew. While its Hebrew origins are not derogatory, many people today (myself included) find the word *Goy* to be an insulting way to refer to a person who is not Jewish. I guess there are words like this for every religion—I find them all equally unappetizing, so to speak.

Anyway, my date makes this offensive remark about non-Jews and their eating habits (which, to be honest, I had never heard. I thought it was *my* family that liked free food). To top it off, he calls them Goys. Now, at this early stage of our relationship—about fifteen minutes into our first date—he doesn't know if I am a practicing Jew, if my mom and dad are Jewish or not, if I'm a socialist, communist, or card-carrying ACLU member. In one sentence he has insulted me and every friend I have, Jewish or not. This was not on his JDate profile.

I left quickly after that, half my bagel still untouched. Free food or not, I had lost my appetite.

My Date with the Minister

Okay, maybe dating within my religion wasn't working out for me. There are more than thirty-nine other organized religions I could try, and since the majority of them fell under the Christianity umbrella, I decided to try one of the most popular sites of this sect: ChristianCafe.com. I posted my picture, listed my affiliation as "spiritual, not religious," and before you could say *Divine Intervention* I had scored the equivalent of a date with a Jewish doctor: I was hit on by a minister. A funny, charismatic (not that way), nice-looking minister of a Unitarian-slash-liberal congregation. So far so good. Trusting that he was looking for a date and not a conversion, I decide to have lunch with him.

We agree to meet at a Thai restaurant not too far from either of us. I show up at the designated time, and the restaurant is closed. It's December 24. Who knew a Jew and a Unitarian clergyman couldn't get curry on the day before Christmas?

I wait for my date to arrive, so we can choose another location. I wait.

And wait.

And after twenty minutes, I say bullshit and I leave my card in the door with a note that says something like, "Don't know if you'll see this but if you do, I was here and you weren't."

I head home, annoyed.

About half an hour later, I get an e-mail from the Minister. I'm so sorry, it says, traffic was terrible.

Listen, Christmas Eve is perhaps one of only five days of the year when Atlanta traffic is *not* terrible. I'm not buying it, but I'm not getting into an argument over it, either.

Not a problem, I e-mail back. Good luck.

Can we reschedule? he asks.

No thank you, I say. I sign off.

He e-mails me twice a day for the next several days: Please reconsider. Let's try again. It's just lunch. I'm sorry I was so late.

I don't know why, but I finally agree. I say to myself, *Maybe someday I'll write about My Date with a Minister.* Just to keep things as easy as possible, I suggest the same restaurant.

I show up. The restaurant is open this time, but he's not there. You think the guy would be early this time. I get a table anyway. Being stood up (twice) makes me hungry.

The Minister comes rushing in a few minutes later. Breathlessly, he begins telling me about the argument he just had with his ex-wife about child support.

This is not a good sign.

Oh, and he doesn't actually have an ex-wife. He has a wife. They are just recently separated. Now, I don't have a strong opinion on this—if two people are separated and everyone is moving on and the divorce is just a matter of timing, I'm okay with this. But I wonder if the rules are different for Ministers.

He continues to gripe about what this divorce is going to cost him, and then he jokes that this may be the only date I've ever been on where the man pays in food stamps. I know he's just trying to be amusing, but for some reason I can't find my amusement center.

We order, and since he brought it up, I ask him the reason he and his wife are divorcing.

"I want passion," he says. "There's no passion."

I can understand what the Minister is saying, but I'm having a hard time with his, well, self-righteous attitude. This is probably why they tell you not to talk about your divorce on a first date— you're likely to sound shallow, critical, and disagreeable. With no past dates to balance out his personality, I can't help wondering if he's shallow, critical, and disagreeable.

Knowing that matchmaking is basically a prerequisite for any self-respecting female member of a church (or synagogue, for that matter), I say, "Well, your congregation must be chomping at the bit to fix you up with women in the community."

"Yes, they are," he says, "just not soon enough for me. They think I should wait until my divorce goes through, but I don't want to wait anymore. I want passion in my life *now*."

> This is probably why they tell you not to talk about your divorce on a first date.

To be fair, he is known for his very impassioned speeches from the pulpit. So maybe for him, passion really is his life. Still, I'm pretty sure he's using *passion* as a euphemism here.

"It makes it difficult," he says. "I can't even date in my own neighborhood. I have to go outside the city limits because my congregants might think it was inappropriate."

I remember, then, that he didn't have a picture of himself posted on ChristianCafe. He had sent me a photo later, after I had answered the initial e-mail he sent me through the site. Before that, he had only told me that he was a known figure in the community and that I shouldn't be shocked.

I wasn't. I don't shock easily.

"It's not easy," he says.

I imagined it wasn't—no divorce is. But I didn't have the answers to his dilemma. I was just a first date, not a praying member of his congregation. I didn't want to offer an opinion or make any judgment, because by the time I was on the noodle salad, I knew that I didn't want to go on a second date. Click. Chemistry. Passion. Call it what you want, I wasn't feeling it. But that's okay, it's just dating, remember?

We finish our lunch and the check comes. Because he had lamented about the cost of divorcing and joked about food stamps, I offer to pay for my half of the lunch. I was actually just being polite; I did not expect to be taken up on my offer. That's no one's fault but my own.

He waves his hand over the check, back and forth, and says, "No, no, no, no, no, okay."

And with that he pulls back his hand and slaps down $10 on a $20 check. I am not lying. How could I? I'm out with a Minister.

I put down $15 to cover the tip and get up to leave. I am no longer annoyed. I am incredulous. Okay, and maybe a little annoyed. This is, after all, the second time I've come out to meet him, and he had clearly been the one to ask me out. Look, in today's dating world, I totally believe in sharing the costs of dating. I'm sure I pay for at least half of the dates I go on, if not more. But a first date that the man himself has arranged? Let me rephrase that: a second date after he's blown off the first one? Call me crazy.

We walk to our cars in the parking lot and the Minister says, "I'd like to see you again."

On second thought, call *him* crazy.

I shake his hand and shake my head and say, "I had a lovely lunch. But no, I don't think so. Thank you, though." I give him a really nice smile and get into my car. This was me employing one of the greatest things I learned while dating: the Art of Saying No. Simply, nicely, firmly. It's not genius, but please read it before you go on your next date. (It's in chapter 8.)

> "I had a lovely lunch. But no, I don't think so. Thank you, though."

The Minister e-mailed me a few more times, asking me if I was sure about that second date (I was) and if I was happy with my religious affiliation. (Ha! I knew it! He was hoping for a convert.) I did not answer him, and for this I hope I do not rot in hell.

A few weeks later I saw the Minister out with a woman at a restaurant near where I live.

Jeez, when he said he had to date outside his neighborhood, I didn't think he meant mine.

Damn. And that was one of my favorite restaurants.

I e-mailed and chatted with men on a couple of other "religious" dating sites, and I went on several more dates. I even went to a few "Hebe-hops" (Jewish parties) and "Bible and Beer" socials (Christian events). These events are fun in my city if you are a guy—any guy, any age, any occupation. The women seemed to outnumber the men about five to one and the madness is like the half-yearly sale at Nordstrom.

In the end, I didn't have much spiritual-dating success, although I did meet one guy I liked a lot and we went out several times. Funny enough, his name was Luke, and he was one of the few guys on JDate who wasn't Jewish, but who just happened to like dating Jewish women.

He took me to his office Christmas party.

Tip 5: Just because you're on a site that puts religion first, don't assume everyone on it follows the golden rule. Be as cautious with whom you meet, where you go, and what you say as you would on any other site.

Luckily, I tried a lot of other sites (and I have the scars and stories to prove it). But no matter which sites you choose, everyone wants to know how to get started. I've taken the most frequently asked questions from my post-divorced, e-challenged girlfriends and covered them in the next chapter. Remember the first time a friend talked you into doing something fun but scary? Like jumping off the diving board or shaving your legs? Well, I figure we're all in this together, and I'm here to jump with you.

Chapter 6
Setting Yourself Up Online

DATING ONLINE IS THE FASTEST WAY TO GET BACK OUT THERE and back on top of your dating game. If you've never done it before, I know it seems a little weird, scary, strange. It is. But only in the beginning. Once you get into it—and *let* yourself get into it—it seems pretty normal, like networking at a convention of available men. Of course, like any new venture, there are things to learn and know and test and try. It also takes a lot of time . . . and so you have to give it some time. In this chapter, I'm going to try to take you from conception to . . . *proliferation.*

My first suggestion is to Google "top dating sites" and read about them. Some of the sites you've never heard of before might be just right for you. The first site I chose was based on where I was in my post-divorce mind-set—not looking for anything serious. Over time, your goals may change, so your site selection may change, too. Keep exploring, but start somewhere.

Tip 1: Before you do anything, such as create a profile or post a picture, spend time on the site to learn what works for other people. Most sites offer tips, blogs (online articles), and forums (discussion groups) full of advice that can increase your chances for good matches. The sites do this because they *want* you to be successful. They like your membership, they like your testimonials, they like watching their matchmaking statistics go up. Read what the experts have to say. Also, look over the profile templates and writing examples that the sites provide—then you'll know if someone's profile is truly clever or if they copied and pasted it from the profile pros.

Tip 2: Start smart. Dating sites such as Match.com offer excellent safety tips, based on input from thousands of men and women, health and safety professionals, and—my personal favorite— therapists. There are also entire Web sites and blogs devoted to dating securely: Check out the basics from Liz Kelly of Smart Man Hunting or onlinedatingmagazine.com for more in-depth info. Do yourself, your body, and your future a favor and read these. You'll learn things about dating safely that will make you more paranoid than you've been in years.

Tip 3: When you join a Web site, do not use your actual name as your profile name. Instead, pick a **screen name** that sounds inviting and describes something about you. Take your time with this and look around the site to see what names other people use, because your screen or profile name is one of the first descriptions of your online identity. And try not to be too aggressive. "Proveit122" or "Mankiller99" is not a very friendly thing for a guy to have to type in the "To:" field of an e-mail.

Tip 4: Set up an anonymous e-mail account that does not reveal your first or last name. Yahoo!, Hotmail, Gmail—almost any service will allow you to choose how your name appears to others. It can be the same as your profile name or something different. Pick something you like, something that's easy to remember, something that makes people think of you. This is the e-mail you will use when you begin to "talk" with guys offline—after you have spent time e-mailing and getting to know them within the dating site. (See "My Hierarchy of Getting to Know You" in chapter 7.) Even when you've taken the step to offsite e-mailing, you don't want to give out your actual name yet. Maybe ever.

> You don't want to give out your actual name yet. Maybe ever.

Tip 5: Include instant messaging (IM) on your new anonymous e-mail account. You will be IMing soon, and the same rules apply for your anonymity. (The name you choose for your new e-mail account from Tip 3 will also be the name that appears on other people's IM **friends list.**) I love IMing—so much so that I devoted most of chapter 7 to it. You will have to learn IM shorthand and acronyms. It's kind of like writing for the classified ads—no capital letters, very few vowels. There are some great sites that list the most popular acronyms and their meanings. Try imacronyms.com or aim.com/acronyms.adp. If you still can't decode someone's message, try acronymfinder.com. If it's not here, then the guy's just making shit up. I'm sorry to inform you that yes, you have to take a few language classes to date in your own country, no matter what country you're in.

Tip 6: Before you create your online profile, check out the competition. That's right, view the *women* on the site who are in your age group and zip code, and see what they look like, what kinds of pictures they post, what they say in their profiles. These are the women who will show up as "matches" (along with you) to the guys online who are seeking women in your age/zip code category. (Some of the initial matching is done solely by demographics.) When you peruse other profiles, take note of the descriptions you like, the pictures that appeal to you, and what seems to appeal to others. (How do you know what appeals to others? Well, on some sites you can see how many friends—and what kind of friends—a person has. This is sort of an indication of how "popular" a person is.) Your goal is to make your profile and picture stand out—in a good way.

Tip 7: Viewing: Turn it off or keep it on? A lot of people don't realize that when you view a guy's profile (or a woman's, for that matter), *your* profile shows up on *his* homepage to show that you viewed him. You can make viewing private if you want to, then browse all you want and no one will know. If you are checking out the female competition, you might want to do this—although personally I never care if women see that I'm viewing their profiles. If you make viewing private while searching men, that's okay, too, but realize that a lot of men look to see who has viewed them. ("Who has viewed you" shows up in their inbox or home page.) You won't show up if you make viewing private. On the other hand, if guys see your picture on their homepage and they like it, they will probably check out your profile, and maybe send you a **flirt** or an e-mail through the site. Keeping your viewing turned on is one way to get a guy's attention without taking any other action.

Tip 8: You can play with your profile settings. You can go into your profile **settings** and change your viewing status at any time. In fact, you can change all sorts of settings whenever you like. For example, if you're taking a break from dating, you can hide your profile completely so no one even knows you're on the site. Then you can look all you want in total privacy. But this also means you will have to make all the initial contacts. You can turn off viewing **privacy** for a few minutes, and then change it back to on. There was one guy I kept viewing to see if he was still online, if he had changed his status in any way, if he had added friends or pictures. Sometimes I didn't want him to know how many times a week I viewed him, so I'd turn off the viewing setting. Yes, this gives you the opportunity to stalk in private. I'm cool with that. See what options you have when you are setting up your profile, and just remember you can change your selections anytime depending on how you want to use the site.

Tip 9: Learn how to cancel your membership. The sites make it very easy to sign up and get on; on some sites it's a little more difficult to get off. Search for the "How to Cancel Your Membership" paragraph in the terms and conditions or FAQs, and print it out, file it in your "dating folder" (yes, set up a dating folder), and mark your calendar for the day that your membership will expire (or a few days before). If you no longer want to be on the site—or you haven't used it for a while and forgot you were even a member—you have to cancel or you may be automatically renewed and charged for another ninety days or more. (What else do you keep in your dating folder? Print out your site receipt, password, and user name. See Tip 11 for more filing fodder.)

Tip 10: Be the first to send an e-mail. Sites make it easy to say a quick hello; you can flirt, wink, or choose a pre-written intro or reply. This is fast but doesn't necessarily achieve your desired result—that is, a guy's reply. If you're really interested in someone's profile, WTF? Send an actual e-mail on the site. Dating stats show that women get 50 percent more replies when they e-mail first. I have no idea why this is, it just is.

> **Women get 50 percent more replies when they e-mail first.**

Tip 11: Track your favorite candidates. In the virtual world there are more men online than women, which typically means that women receive an abundance of e-mails. You probably won't have time to respond to all of them. That's okay. Men pretty much understand this—it's why they send out so many e-mails in the first place. You'll need to set up some sort of system to keep track of who you like, who you've talked to, what you've talked about. You can write notes in an online document or a paper-filled notebook or on a napkin. My friend Caryn prints out the profiles of men she's interested in and makes notes on them (and sometimes draws devil horns or writes obscenities). I keep a printed list of men's profile names and what their real names are, what they do for a living, what we've talked about—just so I have a quick reference. You may laugh or scoff now, but wait until you're talking to three men named Rob, Robert, and Rod and you're trying to keep them all straight! You'll find your own best system as you go, but at least create a system. Once you've begun tracking your favorites, I recommend deleting all the e-mails that you're just not interested in; then sift through the rest and make a top-tier and second-tier list. Next, e-mail the guys at the top of your list and start mingling! But first you have to create a place for the guys to come . . . on to Creating a Profile.

Tip 12: Oh yeah, and don't do anything too stupid, even online.

Creating a Profile That Attracts Quality, Not Crazies

People say that guys are visual, but girls are, too—we're just visualizing different things. The truth is that online profiles with a photo get viewed 80 percent more often than profiles without pictures. So if you're wondering if you really have to post a photo, the answer is "Only if you want to get dates."

Even if you write a hilarious, witty, or eloquent description of yourself on your profile, none of it speaks-and-piques like a photo. Most women I know won't even respond to a man's e-mail if he doesn't have his picture posted, and many men feel the same way.

> Do you really have to post a photo? Only if you want to get dates.

I know, lots of people don't have pictures on their computer or don't know how to **upload** them. I had to go through a steep learning curve, and some of you will, too. Online dating takes some time, some effort, a little knowledge, a little planning. Damn, sounds a lot like a relationship.

In addition to a photo, I have often thought it would be fun to post a "first-date video" on your profile. Then you could have your first date over with. On your video you would show off your first-date outfit, which would show off your best assets. You would go to your favorite pub and say, "This is where we'd go. Those are my girlfriends from the gun club watching from the other side." Maybe you share your funniest childhood story or your latest sports victory. You do not bash the president or your ex. Then you wave good-bye and say, "I'll call you." And voilà! The first date is over. On to the second date, which is so much more comfortable.

But since a first-date video is probably not going to happen, you have to post your picture if you want guys to click on your profile and e-mail you.

A Thousand Words: Your Profile Pictures

Now, don't start pulling photos from your college spring break trip or the decade of your skinny clothes. Think this through. This is like product branding, and yes, you have to have truth in advertising. What do you want your pictures to say? What's your best look—little black dress or low-rise jeans? Think about your best features and make sure they are front and center. And unless you're missing your two front teeth, *smile* in your pictures. This is the number-one quality men mention when they decide whether or not to e-mail a woman. Hey, that's what they *say* . . . it may not be all they're thinking. Here are a few tips about posting your profile pictures:

> This is the number one quality men mention when they decide whether or not to e-mail a woman.

Tip 1: Your pictures need to look like you and be recent. You will eventually meet your online suitors *offline* and they will not be happy if you misrepresented yourself. I once met a guy for a date whose online picture must have been ten years old. The guy I thought I was meeting was tall and slender, with longish hair and a nice smile. The guy flagging me down in the restaurant was tall, wide, and bald. I am serious. And he was smoking—actually smoking while he was greeting me. There went the great smile. He might have been a nice guy, but I didn't stick around long enough to find out, because I was less than thrilled that he wasn't honest about his pictures. Men say it happens to them all the time, too, and it makes them just as mad. It's courteous to post the real deal. The bait-and-switch doesn't work, and it just wastes everybody's time.

Tip 2: Your main photo should show the best you. Take off the sunglasses. Don't post your Halloween picture. Don't crowd your photo with other people so he's not sure which one is you. Your first photo should be just *you,* looking your finest.

Tip 3: Smile. I have received more than 6,000 e-mails and I bet more than half of them have said, among other things, "I like your smile." When a guy sees you smiling, he thinks you seem easy to be with (not that way. Well, maybe that way). And he knows that you've been happy at least one time in your life.

Tip 4: Look damn good. All the other women on the site want to look better than you. Screw that. Put on a little makeup, brush your hair, wear what makes you look and feel great. This is branding, remember?

Tip 5: Have a friend take your picture. Do *not* do one of those self-portraits where you stretch out your camera-holding hand and shoot your own picture. That won't work for this. Make a date with a friend to come over and take pictures of you specifically for your profile. Choose a couple of different outfits: one dressed up, one dressed down, and one that shows off your best feature (eyes, smile, legs, whatever). You don't need an entire photo album—just a few to give everyone a taste of who you are.

Tip 6: Beware of your background. People will see whatever is behind you in the photo: the picture over the fireplace, the dishes in your sink, the kids lurking in the doorway. Seriously, you do not want to take your own picture in your bathroom mirror. I've seen pictures of guys posing in their bedroom and behind them is a huge pile of clothes, a jar of Vaseline on the nightstand, and an unmade mess of a bed. I'm serious! It would be hilarious if it weren't so gross. Don't even get me started on **Web cams** and *those* backgrounds.

Tip 7: If you have a pet, put it in one of the photos with you. But do keep the whole pet thing in perspective. I love animals, but not everyone feels the same way about sleeping with a ninety-pound Lab. If "must love dogs" is one of your non-negotiables, certainly make it part of your profile. Just try not to refer to your pets as your children, your best friends, or anything other than pets. Not in print, anyway.

> Not everyone shares your view of sleeping with your ninety-pound Lab.

Tip 8: I do not recommend putting your kids (or your nieces or nephews or neighbors' kids) **in any of your photos.** People seem split down the middle on this one; I'm not. I think it's appropriate to mention in your profile that you *have* kids or that you *want* kids; I would just protect their privacy by not posting their latest Little League team picture. Remember, anything you post online can be viewed by anyone else online, and there are tens of millions of us.

Tip 9: Just because guys are visual, you still need a paragraph or two that describes you. You'll want to put some thought into this for that one guy who actually reads what you've written. Some sites even offer professional profile writers (for a fee, of course) or templates so you can pick descriptions of yourself from column A, favorite activities from column B, turn-ons and turn-offs from column C, and so on. This is a fine place to start, but plan to revise your profile later as you get more comfortable on the site and learn what's working for you and what's not. Believe me, you will not be the only person on the site who selects from the template: "If I were a car, I'd be a red convertible." Overall, your profile should be on the brief side, upbeat, friendly, witty if you are. Avoid sounding needy, desperate, or arrogant.

Tip 10: Don't post anything too stupid.

Chapter 7

A Girl's Gotta Have a Great Tool

THERE ARE A LOT OF GREAT METHODS FOR COMMUNI-CATING online: chatting, ICQ (shorthand for "I Seek You"), and, my personal favorite, IMing (instant messaging, as in AOL, Yahoo!, and MSN Messenger). I like IMing because it's the closest thing to a face-to-face conversation that you can have without opening your mouth. It happens in real time (hence, "instant") by typing to your friends in a small online window. Unfortunately, when I first tried it, it was as if English was my *second* language. I only understood about half of what anyone was saying. That's because IM uses shorthand that mostly involves abbreviations, words with no vowels, and keyboard symbols (emoticons) that when combined creatively represent feelings, jokes, and innuendos. So, someone would type "brb" and then I wouldn't hear from them for, like, an hour, and I'd be wondering what happened. That's because *brb* means "be right back." Or someone would say something sarcastic and then type ;) and I was supposed to know that was a wink.

> It's the closest thing to a face-to-face conversation that you can have without opening your mouth.

Okay, those are pretty easy. How about when someone wrote "TDTM" and I replied, "Sure." *Great.* It means "Talk Dirty To Me." Then there are the people who *only* talk in symbols. Okay, I get that :-X means "big kiss"; :-J means "tongue in cheek." But come on— :-< means "forlorn." Who even uses the *word* forlorn, much less the symbol for it? People who know a thousand of these symbols scare me. They may be funny, but they're still scary. How much time are they spending on this?

I knew I had to educate myself if I had any hope of IMing with intelligence, and today I admit that this is my preferred way of getting to know someone before spending even one hour on a date. With IM, I can determine if a guy has a brain and how quickly it works; whether or not he has a sense of humor (or a funny friend nearby telling him what to write); whether he has manners or immediately asks if you're wearing underwear. And because I am a writer, I have a distinct advantage in the IM medium: I type really fast. In one evening I can go through four or five potentials. \o/ (Hooray!) Take into account that you can also send and receive pictures via IM, and I can practically have a first date without leaving my laptop.

Be Wary of the Internet's Immediate Intimacy

There is one, um, *downside* to these online chats. Women ask me all the time why guys they meet online get sexually explicit after just a few e-mails or instant messages. I wish I had the answer to this, but then I'd have figured out what makes the entire male gender tick, and I'd be off accepting the Nobel Peace Prize or something instead of writing this snarky little post-divorce dating book and then where would we be? (Wait, I *have* figured out what makes the entire male gender tick. brb . . .)

Sexual conversations do happen quickly online—whether you meet on eHarmony, Christian Cafe, Match.com, or Adult Friend Finder. People start telling you trippy stuff and showing you risqué photos as if we all dated in dog years and every message equals seven years. So by the third e-mail (do the math, that'd be twenty-one years), some guy is asking, "What r u wearing?" or "Where is the strangest place you've ever had sex?" or "Do u have any naked pictures? If u send one I'll send one two [*sic*]."*

You haven't even met the guy and he's asking you things you've never told anyone.

This is definitely a Ripley's trend—strange but true. I've spoken with many experts (not just my friends but *real* Internet experts), and they tell me that the anonymity of cyberspace makes people say things, send things, and upload things that they would never do in person.

And here you are, in front of your computer, saying to yourself, *This guy thinks I'm going to answer him when the only things I know about him are:*

- His screen name is Hotstuff;

---

* *Sic* is an editing term that comes from the Latin word for "yes" or "thus." It means that this is not a typo on my part or the part of my publisher; this is actually how it appears in the original (the way the guy wrote it). I think *sic* covers it perfectly.

- He clearly doesn't know the difference between *to, too,* and *two;*

- His Web cam is on 24/7 (and is that really what his living room looks like?); and

- Okay, he has nice abs.

I don't know, maybe this kind of online banter is the equivalent of booty calls.* The guy is merely thinking, "Maybe I'll get lucky." And a lot of guys—and girls—are willing to play.

But if you are *not* looking for online playtime, I would simply claim a lost DSL connection and **appear invisible** on your IM list for the next week or so. I think this is why we have visible lists of our online friends or buddies in the first place—so we can see who's trying to IM us and ignore the people we don't really want to talk to. I would be careful of engaging in anonymous online conversations that take a hard sexual turn. You never know who is really behind that charming emoticon. It could be some pervert who's saving and storing your pictures for his own private

---

*A booty call is a call you receive from a guy very late at night (or technically, early in the morning). Usually it's from someone you've slept with before or are currently sleeping with but with whom you don't have a serious relationship. The booty call often comes after the caller has been out drinking—sometimes with the guys, sometimes with another girl—and he's calling because he's hoping to get lucky. Hence, booty = treasure, jackpot, gold. Real-life example: When your girlfriend gets a text at 2:00 a.m. and says "I gotta go," you can bet it's a booty call. Whether this is flattering or foolish behavior is purely in the eyes of the booty callee.

pleasure—or worse, it could be an ex with a grudge who is mass e-mailing everything you say to your fifty closest friends and family or posting it on revenge.com.

The "cute guy who works at a law firm" could be half of a swingers couple who IMs single females as cyberotic foreplay. Or the one that really gives me nightmares, it could be Mrs. Schydeemantle, my first-grade teacher, who always said she was keeping her eye on me . . .

The best advice I've heard is not to write or send anything that you wouldn't want your mother (or your boss, your ex, your best friend) to see. What goes online stays online.

> What goes online stays online.

Now, it wouldn't be fair to imply that this is only a man-thing. My friend Adair told me that he met a woman on a dating site, had a few e-mail and IM conversations, and then, wanting to progress to the next stage, asked if he could call her. The woman IMed him back and said that she wasn't ready for phone, but she'd send him some recent pictures.

She sent one of herself on the beach, one of herself with some friends at a party, and one of herself topless.

Not ready to talk by phone but ready to show you her rack?

My friend was like, "No problem. We don't have to talk by phone yet. Just keep sending half-naked pictures and we'll get along just fine."

Men don't have online sexcapades sewn up; it's just creepier when they do it.

My Hierarchy of Getting to Know You

Getting to know someone through online dating is a step-by-step process. It's different (and slower) than getting to know someone at work or the gym because, remember, you have no idea who the person behind the profile really is. Here is my recommended progression for getting to know a guy online:

Step 1: Search the profiles. You can search for men by general descriptors such as age, location, race, and status (single, divorced, never been married), or refine your search with a long list of options: income, height, weight, smoker/nonsmoker, drinker/nondrinker, kids/no kids, and so on. As a first step I recommend that you look at all the men who meet your non-negotiables and your age range, and whose picture and profile you like. This should keep you busy for a few days at least.

Step 2: E-mail within the dating site. Once you pick a guy (or several), write and send an e-mail only from your site profile. This keeps your external e-mail addresses private. Don't agree to e-mail people you don't know from your home, office, or anonymous e-mail accounts—yet.

Step 3: E-mail offsite, through your anonymous e-mail account/ address. (See the tips in chapter 6.) This is still a private way to e-mail with your new friends as you're getting to know them. No last names, no addresses.

Step 4: Instant message (IM). As I mentioned earlier, this is my favorite and fastest way to size up a potential date. Is he quick with a response or does he take forever to answer? Is he paying attention or is he chatting with five other women at the same time? Does he give me one-word answers or just the right amount? Is he funny, smart, cynical, arrogant? These are things you want to know before you agree to a first date.

Step 5: Text. This is really just IMing over a cell phone. Be forewarned: He will now have your cell phone number and you will have his. Texting is a great way to stay in touch—but remember, you're still sizing things up. How often does he text you? How long does he take to reply to your texts? Texting can get a little addicting—you've seen people who can't put down their cell phone, texting through dinners and business meetings. I think that with texting, sometimes less is more.

> With texting, sometimes less is more.

Step 6: Talk on the phone. I wait a pretty long time before I do phone; for some reason, it seems like a big step to go from writing to talking. On the phone, it's a little more awkward to end the conversation if you don't like where it's going or something just doesn't click. It's easier on your computer—you can just sign off. And while this should go without saying (and we all know how good I am at that), I just want to point out: *Do not drink and dial.* It is disastrous to call a guy with whom you are only at phone base during, say, a Girls' Night Out, and drunkenly ask if he wants to meet you.

That's why IMing is safer; it's very hard to type with a drink in one hand.

Step 7: Meet in person. Make a date for coffee or a drink. Be sure to tell your date that you have about an hour in between other commitments. That way, if it's not working out, you can politely leave for your prior commitment and he will not necessarily feel as if you are getting the hell out of there as fast as you can. Even if you are.

Step 8: After all this . . . meet for dinner. Most of my friends say they know early in the first date whether or not there will be a second date. If everything clicks, make a date to meet again and see if you both can sustain the ease, the chemistry, and a conversation for several hours. This is more than I can manage with my mother.

Step 9: Now you are on your own. Of course, if you have a great dinner date but he doesn't call you, IM you, or answer your texts, this will be infuriating and confusing . . . and par for the course. Do not use his e-mail, IM, or cell phone for any personal revenge or to "teach him a lesson." These are tools, not weapons of mass destruction.

Step 10: Don't do anything too stupid.

> See if you both can sustain the ease, the chemistry, and a conversation for several hours. This is more than I can manage with my mother.

Glossary of Online Terms

appear invisible—On most dating sites you have visibility options in your account settings; you can either "hide your profile" (appear invisible) or "show your profile" (everyone on the site can see it). When your profile is hidden, only you can see it—it's not available to anyone else. However, you can still search for men, view *their* profiles, and send e-mails through the site. (Usually you *cannot* send a wink when your profile is hidden. I honestly don't know why.) When your visibility is on, the men you visit will see your photo pop up when they click "Who has viewed me?" A lot of people like this passive way of saying hi. You can also see the men who viewed *you* while your profile was visible, even if your profile is now hidden.

chat—Refers to two or more people "talking" (typing) in real time over the Internet. It's similar to instant messaging, but *chat* often refers to people communicating in an online chat room.

chat room—An area within a Web site, which brings together people with similar interests or who live in the same geographical area. You can usually see the profile names of everyone who is in the chat room (and you'll hear a *ping!* each time a new person enters). You can also see the running conversation among everyone who is chatting. This shows up in real time, line by line, on your screen. Most chat rooms allow you to post pictures; some allow Web cams and video uploads. It's fun, but it can get a little risqué. Be cautious about the information you share.

emoticon—This is an abbreviation for "emotional icon." An emoticon is a combination of keyboard symbols that creates a facial expression or symbolizes a feeling. The most famous emoticon is the smiley face, but IMers have created thousands of others. The smiley face is created using a colon and a right-side parenthesis **:)** Tilt your head to the left and look at it sideways—see the eyes and the smile? Other popular emoticons include **:(** (sad); **;)** (wink); **:D** (big grin); **:-O** (uh-oh); **:-)~** (sticking tongue out or drooling—often meant in a sexual way).

flirt—Different sites have different ways for you to quickly show someone you're interested. If you see a guy you like, but you're not ready to send an email, click on the **flirt** icon. The guy you "flirted" will see it as soon as he signs on. It's a fast way to say, "Hi, I might be interested" without having to say, "Hi, I might be interested." Other sites let you click "wink," "show interest," "put on hot list" . . . there are lots of ways to connect with just one click.

friend or buddy list—You instant message (IM) people by adding their screen names to your "buddy list" (also called a friend list or messenger contact list). When one of your friends signs onto his computer (and IM program), his name automatically appears in your friends list as "online." (We can also sign on as invisible and then no one knows we're on.) You'll also see when someone on your list logs out or times out; they might leave a message next to their name such as "brb" which means "be right back."

IM—Stands for "Instant Messaging." It's an online conversation between two people that takes place in real time. Each of you types your side of the conversation in an online window on your respective computers. The conversation shows up line by line. Your screen name and whatever photo you've uploaded are displayed in the IM window, too.

privacy—See "appear invisible"

profile—A profile is your online description and home page. It typically includes your screen name, your pictures, a couple of paragraphs about you (hopefully written in a unique and interesting way), and the qualities you are looking for in a match. You typically select these qualities from a generic list of possibilities, such as turn-ons, body type, age, interests, religion, location, etc.

screen name—A screen name is a nickname or an alias; the name you select to appear on your profile. (It could also be your IM name and/or the name you use on your anonymous email account.) Because you will be talking to strangers, your screen name should not include any personal information—do not use your real first or last name; do not put your city or your age. Research shows that playful, flirty names rank highest by men and women. Avoid sounding needy, bored or arrogant.

settings—When you sign up as a member of a dating site, you'll have all sorts of options in your account settings: privacy, email alerts, automatic renewal, edit your profile, delete pictures, etc. You can go into your account and change your settings at any time, cancel or renew your membership, change your status or profile, block another user from viewing you. After you've been on the site for a week or so, go back to your account settings and make sure everything is set the way you want it, now that you know what you're doing.

upload—Electronically transfer a file, picture, or video from one place to another. If you want to upload a photo of yourself to your profile page, for example, the photo must reside on your computer or on an external device that you can plug into your computer. For instance, you can upload a photo directly from your digital camera.

view—View refers to a privacy setting on your dating site account. You can choose to have viewing "turned on" in which case people will see that you have viewed them; or you can choose to turn it off, in which case they won't have a clue.

Web cam—A Web cam is a small digital camera that attaches to your computer or is built right into it (typical on later-model laptops). You can use a Web cam to stream or upload videos, or have a "live video chat" with someone over the Internet. Many dating sites support live Web cam chats and video streaming.

Chapter 8

We Screen for Marrieds and Felons

YOU WILL SOON SEE THAT EACH DATING WEB SITE TRIES to differentiate itself from the others, advertising its features in a way they hope will resonate with the kind of people they want as members. Below, in bold, is the advertisement TRUE.com sent to me, in *my* inbox. I added my thoughts (in parentheses) to their ad's selling points:

- **Over 19 million singles.** (I should be able to find one or two who still have some of their hair, and most of it on top of their head.)

- **Connect with women near you.** (Well, I'm staying open-minded, but if you have nineteen million singles, I'm hoping that at least nine and a half million are men. If I go through all of them and still have no luck, then "connecting with women near me" might be something I should consider.)

- **Chat with women live.** (All right, now I'm getting a complex that you think I won't possibly find a man who wants to date me, much less chat with me, so I'll have to resort to chatting with women—live. And just for the record, is there a "chat with women on a time-delayed basis"?)

The final selling point from TRUE.com is this:

- **We screen for marrieds and felons.** (I find it interesting that they put these two in the same category . . . But when they say they *screen* for marrieds and felons, do they mean they pick the best of the marrieds and felons to put on their site? Is that how they get nineteen million members in the first place?)

Because I've been online dating for about 125 weeks, I've had some, um, *interesting* experiences and some that were really remarkable. A few of the people I've dated have remained good friends. A few of them caused me to change my cell phone number.

> **A few of the people I've dated have remained good friends. A few of them caused me to change my cell phone number.**

My first post-divorce, met-him-online relationship was hot, fast . . . and ultimately horrible. He was married, but I didn't learn this for quite a while. Did I mention that I'm a black belt in denial? This is one of the murkiest areas of online dating—people do, say, write, and post anything they want—and if they are good at deception this is their nirvana. If they find someone trusting and naive, it can go on for months. We freshly divorced women are often too new to dating to recognize when we're being duped. That's why we have to educate ourselves, be wary to the point of suspicion, cautious bordering on paranoid. Suffice it to say I learned some of these things a little too late.

But now I subscribe to the X-Files "trust no one" approach to dating.

Of course, the best way to get over a man is to date another man, right?

So a few months after my disastrous right-out-of-the-gate guy, I went on a date with a guy I met on TRUE.com. After all, they screen for marrieds. And felons.

Any Dream Will Do

I liked Bruce. Bruce liked me. But after a few dates, Bruce casually stated that he bet I'd be moved into his house within the year. He did not even take offense when I blurted out, "*That* will never happen!" He laughed. He was sure. He loved that we had this extremely funny "how we met" story—a story we learned only after a few dates. A story he dreamed about telling "our" grand-children. Here it is:

When Bruce asked me where I lived, I told him the name of my neighborhood. (There I go again, breaking my own dating rules.) He said he knew my neighborhood; his ex-in-laws used to live there, but had moved a few years ago. I didn't think much about it. There are two hundred homes in my 'hood.

Then Bruce picked me up one day and we were shocked to discover that his in-laws had lived right next door. I had been friends with them. I had thrown his ex-father-in-law a surprise birthday party! More importantly, I suddenly realized I had met *Bruce* before. Obviously, he'd been married to my neighbor's daughter—but I really didn't know much about her other than the admirable fact that she had the guts to call off her first wedding a week before it happened. I knew this story from her parents. I also knew that a year or so later, she found the man of her dreams and was ecstatic. This man was Bruce. (Unfortunately, their dreams did not make it past the reality-check.)

It gets better. I was actually at Bruce's wedding reception with my then-husband. I was a guest of my neighbors, but we came late so I never actually saw the bride and groom that night. Still, I was there. This was indeed a really great story, but not enough to make me want to marry Bruce so I could tell it to our grandchildren.

After a few more dates, I realized that Bruce was not the one for me. I told him that while I really liked him, I wasn't ready for a full-time boyfriend. I tried to explain that he was like the first dress you try on when you're shopping for the prom. You go into the first store, try on the first dress you see, and you love it. But you've only just started trying on dresses and you have lots of other stores to go to, so you can't possibly buy the first dress you try on. Maybe you will come back and buy that dress at the end of the day, laughing and grumbling about how you wasted so much time. But if any of you are shoppers, you know that rarely happens. You try on lots and lots of dresses, and maybe you don't even take a dress home at all that day. Maybe not for weeks or months. Maybe you decide you're not even going to the prom.

Bruce loved the prom dress story, too. He also planned to tell that one to our grandkids. He knew he'd be the exception to my shopping analogy.

But he wasn't.

He was a great guy, but not a great fit for me. He really wanted to be married again, and somehow it felt that any girl would do. In fact, just months after we agreed that we would just be friends, Bruce was engaged. To a woman named Natasha.

> I tried to explain that he was like the first dress you try on when you're shopping for the prom. You can't possibly buy the first dress you try on.

My friend Mimi said she could tell right away that Bruce wasn't the one for me. But then, Mimi's had a lot of practice dating guys who aren't right for anyone. Like the guy we call "Juuuust Yummmm." She met him online and had been out with him a few times. She really liked him, but he had some *quirks.* Like, every time they were driving in his car he'd look over at Mimi and ask, "Are you happy?"

"He'd practically turn his whole body to face me and ask me this question—more than once during the ride," Mimi said. "It was unnerving. First of all, I wanted him to look at the road. That would have made me very happy. So I would say, as fast as I could, 'Yes, happy. Thanks.'"

Then, every time he kissed her, he would murmur, "Yum. Juuuust Yummmm."

"Every time?" I asked.

"Yep."

"Was he trying to be funny? Cute? Strange?" I asked.

"Well," Mimi said, thinking, "he would say it in what I guess he thought was a sexy voice. I know he meant it as a compliment, but all I could think was, *How do I respond to that?* It just gave me the creeps."

After a few more dates, Mimi stopped going out with him. And yes, she's happy.

The Art of Saying No

Then there was the first date I had from Match.com. On his profile he listed his skills as: martial arts instructor, scuba-certified, gourmet cook, mountain climber, water-skier, ballroom dancer— well, you get the idea. I wanted a date for a formal dance in a couple of weeks, so after we chatted online a bit I asked if he'd like to go. He said yes.

He showed up in a tuxedo . . . sort of. No tie, no cummerbund, and his shirt was stained and wrinkled. He told me this was his "chorus uniform" and he hadn't had time since their last performance to get it dry-cleaned. From the scent of the jacket, I was thinking the last performance must have been on a horse farm. At least he said he could dance, I thought.

Sure enough, Robert walked me to the dance floor right away, and as the music started it was all I could do to hang on. He was spinning me, multiple times in a row, then flinging me in an outward arc so I had to catch my balance on the other side of the dance floor. I felt like I was on a *Punk'd* version of *So You Think You Can Dance?*

I tried dancing separately from him but he would grab my hands and give me another whirl. We were bumping into people left and right, and I was wondering if I could break off the heel of my very expensive shoe just to get the hell off the dance floor. That's when it happened. He suddenly put one hand behind my neck, the other hand below my waist, and dipped me—very deep, without any warning.

We fell. We crashed, actually, ending up in a small heap right in the middle of the dance floor. When I finally got up and limped to our table, I told him I thought I would just sit the rest of the night out. In hindsight, dancing might have been better than enduring his tall tales for the next two hours. He talked on and on about scuba trips with barracudas and rock climbing with frozen hands and Brazilian combat fighting with malaria. *I really should have come alone,* I thought. *Instead I brought a schizophrenic Indiana Jones.* How had I missed this through my IM screening process?

I did learn something extremely valuable that night. I learned what I call the Art of Saying No—politely, firmly, and quickly, at the end of the first date. If there are forty million men online, it's best to cut your losses and try again.

> I really should have come alone. Instead I brought a schizophrenic Indiana Jones.

In my Art of Saying No, I typically start off by saying, "Thank you so much for the date tonight. But I really don't think we're a match. I wish you the best in your search." There, nicely done.

That's the greatest thing about Match .com—it's given us a whole new vocabulary for rejection. Instead of saying, "I think you are a [fill-in-the-blank: dork/weirdo/woman-izing bastard]," we can simply say, "We're not a match." Much more ladylike.

> Most of my dates have not read the memo about how to receive the Art of Saying No.

However, most of my dates have not read the memo about how to receive the Art of Saying No. Don't they realize how much courage and grace I have to channel from Audrey Hepburn to pull this off? I would much rather do the cowardly "I'll talk to you soon" thing and then move out of the country.

Instead, some of my dates would challenge me. "How can you tell after just one date?"

"I just can, really, thank you."

"I don't think you gave it a chance," some would say. "I think you're making a mistake," said others.

Now, to be honest, some of my dates were very relieved to hear my Art of Saying No, since I had simply beaten them to the punch. Some dates didn't even wait for my little speech *or* use their own version of the Art of Saying No. They'd just say "Gotta go—I'll call you sometime" in a way I knew they wouldn't.

But for those who would not take a polite decline, I would pull out the ringer—the one-liner I had developed because it felt honest and true, and it was irrefutable.

I'd say, "Just because *we* don't click, please don't let my preferences define you."

I actually mean this, and I've said it to more than one date. It's not about who *he* is but about what *I'm* looking for. In fact, it's true about every guy I've ever dissed in this book. It's not him, it's me.

And you know what? I have to remind myself of that one-liner every time a guy doesn't call, doesn't write, and doesn't want to go out on a second date with *me*.

Chapter 9

A Different Kind of Match

ABOUT A YEAR AFTER MY DIVORCE, I JOINED A DATING SITE called fitness-singles.com. Because dating takes so much time, I thought there must be some way I could combine something I was already doing with meeting guys. I know, I know—a relationship takes a lot of time, too, but at least you're not spending hours searching through pictures and profiles, trying to find what you're looking for.

PlayDates for Adults

So, as I began to wonder what activity I was already doing that I could combine with dating, it hit me—exercise! I spend about four hours a week working out, and I've played tennis for years. (Plus I own some really nice tennis skirts, although I do have to wear those bras that kind of mash my boobs, but I was sure there was an athletic fashion solution for that.)

So I went online to see if there was something like a singles party for tennis players. You know, a round-robin with lots of partners or a game of tennis and beer. Plus, there are lots of opportunities for my kind of pun-y wit to shine during a singles tennis party: Whose balls are these? Want to change partners? That kind of thing. Okay, well, I play better than I banter, and I don't lose a game just to score points. You know what I mean.

So I find fitness-singles.com, fill out my profile, and take a look around. What's nice about this site is that most of the people really do look fit. They're in their shorts and swimsuits and workout gear and they rock climb and kayak and bicycle and trek (whatever that is). But I'm really just looking for a simple tennis match. Oh yeah, and love.

I get a lot of responses right away—apparently a lot of people are comfortable looking for a tennis partner in hopes of leading to something more. After a few days of online chatting and e-mailing, I agree to meet Chad for a drink at my favorite first-date venue.

When I get there he's already at the bar, and he does indeed look pretty fit. He's football-player fit, which is fine, but not exactly the physical type I go for. I like basketball-player-who-mostly-sits-on-the-bench fit—tall with lean muscles that are just about hidden unless you're actually using them. But fit is fit, and that's good. I see that he already has a drink—clear liquid, lime on rim. I assume it's a vodka tonic.

I sit down and we smile and talk about the day, and the bartender comes over to take my drink order. Since this is my first-date haunt, I know the menu by heart. I order a chocolate espresso martini, something the cafe is known for.

My date has never heard of this drink. He asks what's in it. The bartender tells him as he makes it, "Espresso, vanilla vodka, Bailey's, a shot of chocolate."

He sets it down in front of me, and I am anticipating that first delicious ice-cold sip. But before I can lift it to my lips, my date leans over the glass and glances back at the bartender and says, "How many calories you figure are in that thing? About 600? That's like a Big Mac, isn't it?"

> **Before I can lift it to my lips, my date says, "How many calories you figure are in that thing? About 600?"**

I start to grin, thinking it's a joke, but the look on my date's face stops me mid-martini. He's serious. Very serious, as in, *You're not actually going to abuse your fine body with that mixture of sugar-is-the-devil, cow's-milk-dairy, and alcohol, are you?* I think to myself, *This could be the shortest date in history.*

Ignoring his look, I take a sip of my drink and pronounce it delicious. I make up a statistic (which I am prone to do about 80 percent of the time) and say, "Did you know this drink has 20 percent of the recommended daily allowance for calcium? More than a Starbucks low-fat latte."

He seems impressed by this. He didn't consider the vitamin and mineral factor. After all, we met on a fitness site. I wouldn't just be drinking empty calories with no nutritional value. Bone density, that's what it's all about. Remember, I'm a tennis player.

His football-player mentality notwithstanding, he says, "But it does have a lot of sugar."

You are bringing me down, boy, I think, but instead I lick my lips and say in my most syrupy voice, "Mmm-hmmm, it sure does. When's the last time you had something sweet?"

I don't actually mean the double entendre, but I can't help it. And now I can actually see the click going on in his brain: *Girl-flirting alert. Say something witty.*

"Well, you know, even pizza has nutritional value," he says, in what I guess is a fitness fanatic's way of flirting back. "Tomatoes, veggies, antioxidants . . . calcium, vitamin D. The crust isn't so great, unless you get whole wheat."

I nod. I wonder if there is an IQ test along with the BMI (Body Mass Index) on the Fitness Singles site. How did I not see this coming in half a dozen e-mails? He never once mentioned the caloric content of anything we were talking about.

I do what any self-serving, genetically fit woman would do when up against the Arnold Schwarzenegger of dates—I ask him if he'd like to try my drink.

"Uh, sure," he says.

And just like that I've given crack to an ex-addict.

I have no idea when Chad had last sipped chocolate syrup. I don't know if his mom made him cookies after school and let him dunk them in a glass of cold milk, or if she made him eat sliced apples and peanut butter. But I know I ruined him that night.

Chad, being a big guy, had two chocolate espresso martinis in an hour. He became animated, happy, able to discuss things without mentioning either fat content or calories. He even told me that he'd had a hamburger last week—his first in years.

Stick with me, I thought. *I'll have you driving through the Steak and Shake before the night is out.*

But I didn't. I had done enough damage for one night. Recognizing that this was never going to be a match—not even a simple tennis match—I told him I had to go and stepped down off my barstool. He stood to walk me out but his martini glass was still half full.

"That's okay," I said, "stay and finish your drink."

He gave me a kiss then—on the lips, tasting faintly of chocolate milk. He lingered there a moment. I bet he was thinking of his fifth-grade girlfriend.

As I walked outside, I turned to wave. And there he stood. Not looking at me at all.

Instead, he was eyeing the glass display of enormous European desserts.

Game, set, match.

Maybe there's something about playing sports that makes a guy act strange around a girl. Does testosterone go bad? My friend Mimi had a date with a guy who was really into volleyball. Since Mimi is a volleyball player, too, she said they had an instant connection when they met for coffee. She needed a doubles partner for a couple of upcoming tournaments, so she asked him to play. It turned out, he was a good player.

"But every time I would set the ball for him to hit, I'd hear him say, 'Yeah, baby, mmm-hmmm, baby, right there, yeah, that's good, ahhh.'"

You gotta be kidding me.

She said it was like he was having foreplay while they were playing volleyball. And she was dying of embarrassment because the other team could hear him! They'd laugh and tease her and behind his back they referred to him as "Volleyball Orgasm Guy."

Mimi had the last laugh. They won the tournaments. But she said she had to eventually dump him. It was too distracting.

I don't know. I think if they put this guy on the circuit, there could be a whole new surge in volleyball attendance. Something to rival, say, NASCAR. *Is* there a volleyball circuit?

> **Behind his back they referred to him as "Volleyball Orgasm Guy."**

Chapter 10

What to Wear

LAST WEEK I WENT TO DINNER AT A LOW-KEY restaurant with a couple of girlfriends—girlfriends who have been married for years. When I walked in, they said (pretty much in unison), "My God, you look great. Where did you get that cute top?"

I looked down and realized I was wearing my first-date outfit—a pairing of shirt and jeans whose casual chic-ness denied the hours it took me to get the combination just right. It's an outfit that whispers *I wanted to look great for our first date,* but doesn't scream *This took me all day to do.* My goal on a first date is to walk in as if I always look this way, as if I have no idea what you mean when you talk about women who hang out in their pajamas from morning till night and then morning again.

So I explained to my girlfriends, "This was my first-date outfit when I started dating after my divorce. I bet I've worn it almost a hundred times."

"What's that little black thing peeking out?" my friend Pam asked.

"It's a silk camisole—I never wanted to expose all this cleavage right off the bat."

I bent over a little to show her how distracting this might be to a mere mortal man who would be trying desperately not to look at my chest on the first date, because he'd read somewhere that guys should maintain eye contact with a woman or she might get offended.

Honestly, I think I'd be offended if my date *didn't* check out my breasts at least once or twice over the course of an evening. I mean, I've taken the time to display them in a tasteful and attractive manner.

You Never Know Who You Might Meet

Which brings me to the point that my girlfriends made when they noted the fact that they were wearing whatever they put on that morning while I had "gotten dressed." Once you're divorced and open to dating, it's pretty rare that you will go out wearing what you've worn all day. You get in the habit of putting your best foot (or leg or shoulder or breast) forward. *After all,* you think (even though it rarely happens), *you never know who I might meet at the car wash.*

At no time does dressing carry more on its un-padded shoulders than when preparing for a first date. Now, I could write about women's clothes the way some people write about food. In fact, I probably do write about clothes with too much breathy detail in this first-date-outfit chapter. I hope you won't mind. What I want you to know is that dressing deserves your attention. Maybe you could just pretend it's your favorite cookbook.

> Get in the habit of putting your best foot (or leg or shoulder or breast) forward.

Here's the thing about your first-date outfit: It has to achieve just the right balance. You want to look attractive but not slutty. You want to look casual but not sloppy. You want to look hip but not ridiculous. You want to show off your best assets but still be ladylike. And, of course, you need to take into account the venue where you're meeting and what your date is likely to be wearing (although that's not nearly as important as what *you* want to wear).

> You want to look attractive but not slutty. Casual but not sloppy. Hip but not ridiculous.

While this all may sound very complicated, it's actually just a matter of sizing things up.

What is your very best physical feature? Eyes? Legs? Ass? Breasts? Whatever it is, give it star billing. Overall, your goal is to look good. Because when you look good, you feel good, and that shows up as confidence. And confidence, to quote the guys (see chapter 16), is damn sexy.

Your Own First-Date Outfit

As you are getting ready for your first date, you really have no idea if there will be a second date, but you want to make your best first impression just in case, right? So let's say you have great legs. What should your first date outfit include? (No, not stripper shoes, you're getting ahead of yourself.) A skirt. In fact, a nicely fitted, just-above-the-knee skirt with a small slit in back would be perfect. And if you are blessed with beautiful sticks, then you probably wear skirts as regularly as the rest of us wear sweatpants. Pull one out that's not too short and not too tight and pair it with the great shoes you also probably own. (If not, invest in a pair of heels that look great and that you can actually walk in. We've all seen pretty women ruin their entrance by walking on shoes as if they were about to fall over. Don't be a victim, okay?) Now, in your skirt and heels, sit across from your date at the table and pull out your chair slightly farther than you normally would, and cross those legs a little to the right or left—you have just taken full advantage of your God-given gams.

For every woman there is an outfit that accentuates her positives. For my friend Mimi, it is her "ba-BAM" skirt. It's white, falls to mid-calf, and is made of some clingy material that, when draped on her, literally makes men stutter. "I- I- I'm so g-g-g-glad that wuh-wuh-was you when I s-s-s-saw you walk in," they'll say.

> **For every woman there is an outfit that accentuates her positives.**

"I was blessed with a great ass," Mimi says, shrugging. "Ever since I was thirteen, guys have been telling me they love to walk behind me. *Women* even tell me I have a great ass! My ba-BAM skirt shows it off perfectly. I get to look hot without looking trampy. I'm never going to retire that skirt . . . I can imagine myself as an old woman, talking to my granddaughter, holding it up and saying, 'This used to drive the men wild in the nursing home.'"

Mimi says if she's really interested in the guy and she wants to make sure he knows what she's got, she excuses herself, gets up, and walks—slowly—to the ladies' room. "I can practically hear him holding his breath," she says.

For most of us who are blessed with more run-of-the-mill girl-stuff (which, don't get me wrong, is great stuff to work with), I recommend a good pair of jeans. I'm not talking any old pair of Levi's and God-forbid anything acid-washed. You've got to invest in at least one pair of today's designer jeans. They are well worth it, because here's what they do for you:

- They make you look younger. Not younger like you're trying to dress like a teenager, but younger as in cool, confident, energetic. A woman of any age can find the right pair of jeans, I swear. Call me.

- Today's jeans make your legs look longer, especially if you pay the extra twenty bucks to get them hemmed by someone who will put the original hem back on them. This is the cheapest custom alteration you'll ever have. Make sure that you wash the jeans before you hem them (if they can go in the dryer and you plan to dry them this way, do that now, too). And hem the jeans to the shoes that you will wear on all your first dates (flats are fine as long as they're clever, but I recommend heels or a platform on a first date—choose at least two

> You've got to invest in at least one pair of today's designer jeans.

inches). Finally, never hem your jeans too short. Unless you like to wear straight-legged skinny jeans (and you know who you are), let your jeans skim the floor—no shorter. This gives you the absolute longest, most flattering leg. I recommend a slight flare or boot leg (*not* bell bottom) because in addition to giving you long, lean legs, a little width at the hem also makes your waist look smaller. It's some sort of physics thing that works in our favor.

- Jeans make you look sleek, contemporary, and hip—but only if you can actually sit in them. Do not go for jeans with a super-low waist or you'll only be able to wear tops that go down to your hips to cover the panties (or worse, the crack) that show every time you sit down. Also, don't buy jeans that grip you too tight at the waist. Your rolls will roll over the waistband—and this not only looks bad, but will make you feel bad. Jeans that have a slight stretch are the best; look for 2 percent spandex. Yes, I've researched this.

- Jeans are perfect for just about any first-date locale: dinner, dancing, a cup of coffee, a glass of wine, or even an unexpected breakfast.

- So let's recap: With a pair of today's jeans, you get a younger look, longer legs, a smaller waist, a feeling of confidence, a grab-and-go outfit that goes just about anywhere—all for $150 or so. That's cheaper than one application of Botox.

Jeans come in a thousand shades of blue, plus black and brown if you can find them. I am over forty so I will not be wearing the new colored jeans in yellow and coral and purple and turquoise. You go right ahead if you like them and they look good on you. But shoot me if you see me in them.

There are so many back-pocket options, it would take an entire chapter to cover them all. Here are my top jeans recommendations: If you can only buy one pair, make it a dark rinse blue with just stitching on the pockets (no rhinestones, no colored thread). If you can buy two, buy a second pair in another material, such as a brushed velvet or corduroy (these are for fall, winter, and early spring only; don't forget the spandex). This way, if you're not sure that your first-date place allows jeans, you're technically not wearing jeans, but you still get all the booty benefits. In the spring and summer months, there is nothing hotter than a great pair of white jeans—you can wear them until the first frost, really, and if you pair them with light-colored sweaters and scarves and boots, then the new rules are that you can get away with white jeans in the winter. I covet a pair of white corduroys from Hudson Jeans.

And that brings me to my personal favorites. I'm of a certain age where True Religion would just look silly on me (and I don't usually wear thongs, so what would show when I sit down would not be pretty). But if True Religion jeans look good on you, go for them. I'll hate you, but that's okay. They are incredibly flattering. Hudson Jeans are a better choice for my age group and the next generation or two up, and they look a whole lot like True Religion without the need to be supermodel-skinny or have

Victoria's Secret labels on your panties. I am also a fan of 7 For All Mankind (they have the best denim-to-stretch ratio, but a couple of styles tend to have short rises so make sure you can sit in them); Citizens of Humanity (my first designer jean), and AG Adriano Goldschmied. (your butt has to be perfect, though—it takes a certain upper roundness. Check out your backside carefully in the mirror; if you don't have it, move on.). I am a recent convert to jeans by Paige (my newest white pair). A lot of my friends love Christopher Blue—they were their starter designer jeans. They're a little higher in the waist and are clearly not your daughter's jeans; if they look good and make you feel good, that's the jean for you.

You can buy all of these brands at the regular retailers— Nordstrom and Bloomingdale's and Macy's—or maybe your city has a boutique or two that specializes in jeans. Victoria's Secret jeans look great and will save you about 40 percent, but you have to try on each style to see what works for your hip size and leg length. You can also check out discount retailers, such as TJ Maxx and Marshalls. You'll get the same or similar styles for half the price or less. My tip is to try on the jeans at the regular retailers first so you know what they are supposed to look like, then see what the discount stores have. The goal of a great pair of jeans is to make you look sexy. If the bargain jeans don't do that, don't buy them—that's not a bargain.

Remember to buy your jeans tight (they will give) but not binding; they should make your butt look good, so pay attention to how low the pockets are. You don't want to look as if your pockets have landed at the top of your thighs. They need to actually be somewhere on your rear end. Keep trying on brands until you find the designer and style that work for you—there really is a jean for everyone, and I don't say this about all clothing, like bathing suits, for example. Send me a picture when you're in the dressing room. I'll be glad to give you my honest opinion. Really.

And don't forget, ladies, God invented Spanx to make up for childbirth and PMS. It's like a miracle, so don't be afraid or embarrassed to embrace it. I would, however, remove your Spanx in private—your boyfriend does not need to know all your secrets.

So now we have the bottoms . . . what's on top? Well, that's the great thing about jeans. They go with just about anything. My favorite first-date top is something feminine but not fussy, that shows a little but not too much cleavage. That's it. Don't go crazy with color or pattern; choose something that brings out your eyes or skin tone or goes great with your hair.

The top I've worn for the past two years is a delicious light cocoa color with a slightly low neckline that has tiny beads sewn along a whisper of thin chiffon material (see, it's like describing a cake and frosting). Most guys probably don't notice these details because they are running alongside my freckles and that cleavage I mentioned. The material is a lightweight crushed-velvet kind of thing—it's hard to describe but it's unpretentious and feels good to the touch. There's something about guys and their tactile senses—they love to touch soft fabrics, especially when you're wearing them. My first-date top isn't tight (too obvious) and it's not really loose, either (do show your shape). It's feminine, a little romantic, and a little racy. That's what I recommend on a first date: sweet but not too innocent. Unusual but not outlandish. For me, it's the perfect combination—the parts of my personality I like to put forward personified through my outfit.

My final piece of first-date clothing is this really cool, dark brown shawl with soft leather strips sewn along the sides. It sounds cowboyish but it's not; it's just a simple shawl made ultrahip with the suede fringe. Guys have actually commented on it; one of my most recent dates ran his fingers along the fringe more than once, commenting on how much he liked the texture. (It's that soft-touching thing again.) Somehow the coolness of the wrap translates to me being cool. (I know, I just chose it, I didn't make it, but on a first date what you wear is an expression of who you are.) A wrap is a great way to cover up if you start to feel too exposed; and it's an elegant way to make an entrance and slip out of later in the evening. So find something wonderful to wear that you feel good in and that complements who you are.

> That's what I recommend on a first date: sweet but not too innocent.

Keep jewelry simple; hoop earrings typically look good on everyone. A lot of men are weird about women who still wear their wedding ring, but FTS, do what feels right to you. In fact, I wear a ring on my left-hand ring finger that you would never mistake for a wedding band, and I still have guys ask me why I wear it there. But that's okay, talking about it makes for good conversation.

Of course, the best thing you can wear on a first date (and I'm going to sound like your mother on the first day of high school) is your smile. Also your self-confidence, kindness, sense of humor, and brain. A positive outlook outshines anything you have on your body; be ready with an easy laugh, a quick wit, a listener's ear, and a good story or two. You need to have something to say to hold up your end of a first date. That doesn't mean talking about your kids or your ex or your troubles at work. Talk about movies or music you like. Share a cute (and short) story about your family or childhood. I don't usually talk about politics or religion, but I won't shy away from it if the topic arises, either. Some men (and women) see a first date as kind of an interview; that usually sucks. Make yours more fun than that. You can always get up and walk to the bathroom . . .

Underneath it all you should wear great lingerie. My friend Jen says when she wears beautiful bras and panties she feels pretty—whether anyone sees them or not. I shop Target or Victoria's Secret for special occasions—it doesn't have to be expensive to look and feel good. For every day I swear by OnGossamer (makes you look as if you had a boob job without the expense) and I love Le Mystère panties (but I consider them a splurge).

And underneath your underthings you also need to be well groomed—shower, shave, trim, floss, brush, rinse, spit, repeat. You need to smell as good as you look, but be careful with perfumes and hair products. Men will be the first to tell you that less is more. Even if you have on the best fragrance you've ever smelled and people literally stop you on the street to ask what it is, you should use fragrance on a first date sparingly if at all. It can be a total turn-off—shit, it could be the one his ex wears.

Your first-date outfit should be one that makes you look and feel great. When you know you look your best, you don't give it a second thought; your personality and style come through naturally, and you can concentrate on your date and whether or not he's got what you're looking for.

> **When you know you look your best, you don't give it a second thought.**

The good news is, if it's not a match, you can go home and hang up your first-date outfit for next time. After all, no one sees the first-date outfit twice. That's why it's a first-date outfit.

I guess we'd better work on your next-date outfits . . .

Chapter 11

First Dates and Horror Dates

I'M OUT WITH MY GIRLFRIEND GROUP ONE NIGHT AND WE'RE talking about guys (big surprise there) and one woman tells us that a man she recently met asked her to go to Las Vegas on what would essentially be their first date. She wanted to know if we'd think she was crazy if she went.

Well, I hate to use the word *crazy* when *insane* seems so much more appropriate. I'm always a little suspicious of guys who want to impress girls with an elaborate first date. Similar to someone who owns a really fancy sports car, it makes me wonder if he is overcompensating for something. Or maybe he just wants to make sure he gets to show you what's under the hood.

Either way, Las Vegas seems a little too big for the beginning, don't you think? I mean, a first date can go either way—the promise of a possible romance or the emergence of a raving psycho. You want to take a chance on an entire weekend of that?

When a guy pays a girl's way for a weekend, what goes to Vegas stays in Vegas, right? Are you willing to pay the excessive less-than-three-days'-advance-purchase

> A first date can go either way— the promise of a possible romance or the emergence of a raving psycho.

airline ticket price to get the hell out? (I've done this before—trust me, it's worth it, but it will still make you nauseous when your Amex statement comes.)

With a first-date guy, you don't know if he's a gambling addict, a sex addict, a shopaholic, an alcoholic—all things Las Vegas caters to. Heck, no matter where he wanted to take you, you don't know enough about the guy to be with him on a forty-eight-hour first date, do you?

Tales from the Trenches

My ex went all the way to California for a first date, to go skiing with a woman he'd been talking to online for several weeks. They "talked" every day, several times a day, and he felt there was something there. The fact that her pictures consistently showed a flat-bellied navel piercing didn't hurt, either.

She invited him to go to Tahoe for the weekend. Have a good time, I said, as he loaded up skis and boots he hadn't used in ten years. When he got there, he said he could tell within an hour that this was not the woman of his dreams. Within three hours he wasn't sure he even liked her.

First of all, the pictures she'd been sending were at least five years old and fifteen pounds ago. But there was a bigger problem, he said, something that's hard to know about a person until you've spent some time with her. He didn't like her character. It wasn't something he could define easily—she didn't outright lie, cheat, or steal—but as he started to get to know her, he realized she lacked a certain honor that he desires in a girlfriend. Yet he had to spend the weekend with her and try not to look at his watch too often.

> **He could tell within an hour that this was not the woman of his dreams. Within three hours he wasn't sure he even liked her.**

The days weren't too bad because, after all, they had on tons of clothes and were racing downhill in freezing weather and didn't do all that much talking. But at night he said it was downright awkward: It was clear that she wanted to share a room. My ex, who is a master at ignoring sexual advances, managed to sleep alone without pissing her off—too much. She didn't throw him off the gondola or anything. He was very relieved when it was time to go. And he decided to date closer to home from then on.

The point is, a weekend away sounds great—*is* great—with the right person. The right person is not someone you have never been on a date with.

You think my ex's date was bad? One of my girlfriends had a much more revealing first date. She tells the story of a guy who asked her to go hiking. She agreed to meet him at the bottom of a trail about an hour from where she lived, and everything started off fine. He offered to carry her backpack in a gentlemanly but not condescending way, which she politely declined. They walked side by side when they could, and he stepped aside when the trail narrowed to allow her to go first. The conversation was light, interesting, and frequently had them both laughing. By the time they were halfway up the climb, she felt as if this might have the possibility of a second date.

As the climb elevated, the path narrowed, and they were hiking single-file more and talking less. Still, the silence seemed comfortable. She made it to the top of the trail just ahead of him and took in the view, breathing deeply. He had not joined her right away, and when she heard footsteps behind her she turned around to find her date totally naked, arms spread wide, exclaiming, "Isn't this beautiful!"

She told me that she was honestly speechless—that words literally would not come out of her mouth, probably because it was hanging open so wide. Oblivious to her astonishment, her date said, "I thought this would be the perfect place to make love."

Since uncomfortable situations often strike my friend as funny, she tried not to laugh as she said, "You've got to be kidding."

Not exactly what her date was expecting to hear. Needless to say, the hike back down the mountain was not nearly as friendly. Thank God she had met him there and was able to hop in her car and leave.

To me, the strangest part of this first date is that the guy simply assumed my friend would want to have sex—he didn't suggest it, didn't ask her, didn't even kiss her. He just figured that once she saw his, um, *view,* she wouldn't be able to resist. I asked her if in hindsight she could see this personality trait in him. She told me it's harder to spot than you'd think.

Safety Bordering on Paranoia

Since my hope is that you will go on many, many first dates in the coming year(s), I do have a few first-date tips:

Tip 1: Always meet in a public place. You drive yourself there and he meets you there. Be vague when he asks how far away you live or what route you took to get there. If you can find a place where everybody knows your name, that would be even better. Over the course of a year, I met more than twenty first dates at a local cafe not too far from my home but in the middle of a large retail area. I was friends with the owners and manager, and they looked out for me every time. Sure, they were making bets and a few lewd comments behind the bar, but the one time a guy tried to stick his tongue down my throat, there they were, ready to throw him out. If your family owns a restaurant, that would be good. If your family has connections to the mob, that might be even better.

Tip 2: Tell a close friend where you're going and ask her to call you fifteen minutes after the date start time, to give you an out if you need it. Don't answer if everything is going well; you can text her from the bathroom in a few minutes so she knows you weren't abducted. If you do answer because it's *not* going well, be prepared to act shocked and distraught by the "news" you are receiving from the other end of your phone. If you can cry on command, great. Now you have an exit strategy.

Tip 3: Always have an exit strategy. I suggest that you tell your date beforehand that you have another obligation one hour after your date starts. If you're having a good time, you can always call your "other appointment" and postpone it. Let him hear you *postpone* it—not cancel it—just in case the date takes a bad turn.

> Tell your date beforehand that you have another obligation one hour after your date starts.

Tip 4: If you feel uncomfortable for any reason, get out. I find that faking nausea works for me. Another friend of mine fakes a cramp and says she just got her period. She actually says that—guys hate hearing that. Yes, this is the one and only time that I am recommending you fake it. But if you're getting strange vibes, get out—down the mountain, as it were. Be very pleasant, do apologize for cutting the date short, and make sure you don't act like you think he's got some hideously contagious disease. You never want to piss off a stranger—especially one who has your cell number, e-mail address, and IM name, and was maybe expecting a good night kiss.

Tip 5: And if after all this you do agree to go hiking, do not walk in front of him. Otherwise he'll be staring at your ass the whole time and thinking what guys think when they're staring at a girl's ass. Guys are hardwired and connected to their erections. They just come that way. It is hard for them to think when all their blood is flowing below their waist. This is not an excuse for you to forgive them their ignorance or arrogance, it's just a fact. Take it into account when you make a date. Especially in Vegas.

Tip 6: Don't do anything too stupid.

Chapter 12

How Many Dates Until We Have Sex?

NAKED IS A WORD THAT COMES UP A LOT WHEN I'M TALKING to women who are recently divorced. No, we're not discussing switching teams. What we're usually talking about is that moment when the divorce really hits home. When we take off our wedding band for the first time and stow it away in a drawer somewhere (or perhaps sell it to buy a Bowflex).

Some women agonize over removing that ring, that symbol of "he actually loved me enough to pay retail for this." Many women leave their ring on for months or years after their divorce. But for those of us who take it off, or *finally* take it off, we somehow feel naked again. When we glance down and see that the second finger from the left is now bare, we feel exposed, like the first one in a strip poker game who has to remove her bra.

And that brings up another fear I hear from divorced women all the time: "Will I ever be naked in front of a man again?" (And in our heads we're pleading: *Please say yes, please say yes, please say yes.*) Whether you've been with the same man for twenty-five years, ten years, or six months . . . whether you've loved him deeply or resented him fiercely . . . if he's seen you pregnant, peeing, or pre-menopausal . . . the truth is, you've had a certain level of stripped-down comfort with that man. Even the most gym-obsessed women tell me that they worry about "the next first time." I think it has less to do with how hard our bodies are and more to do with how soft our feelings are—feelings of vulnerability that divorce often brings to the surface. And for those of us who were in marriages where intimacy hadn't raised its lovely head in a long time, we wonder whether or not anyone will ever find us desirable again.

Well, I think if we choose to, we *will* be naked again. It may be years before we take it off or years that we decide to leave it on, but more often than you can imagine, the topic of getting down will come up.

> **More often than you can imagine, the topic of getting down will come up.**

I've talked to a lot of women who tell me that guys want to—expect to—hook up at the end of a first date, and they're wondering if they really have to have sex that early in a relationship. Well, first of all, one date does not constitute a relationship (for most of us) and the answer to the question is abso-fucking-lutely *no.* You never *have* to have sex if you don't want to. This is one rule that has not changed: You always have the right to say no, and no means no—whether you are a college freshman, a single mom, a CFO, or anyone in between.

When to Get Naked. Again.

The real question women want to know is: *How many dates should I wait until we do have sex?* Because contrary to what we typically hear, many women who are recently divorced are looking for a casual (sexual) relationship. This is slightly different from men, many of whom are just looking for casual sex (minus *any* reference to a relationship).

I know, women aren't supposed to admit that they don't want a "real" relationship, but hell, if you're just coming *out* of a "real" relationship, you may not be ready to open your heart to a man again. You may be ready to open your arms, though, and, well . . .

I'd say about one-third of the women I spoke to told me they went "a little nuts" right after their divorce. Others decided to go solo for a while. A few decided to ditch the guy-thing altogether and date women. (The ironic thing about that is, it seems to turn men on more than anything a straight woman can dream up.)

Some of the women who are still in their going-a-little-crazy-after-the-divorce phase tell me they've been accused by their lover(s) of "being like the guy"—they don't cuddle after, they don't want to spend the night, they don't call the next day.

"I like the high of being in control," says Jennie, who's been divorced about a year. "I like the power."

This sexual freedom is new for Jen; she was married for fifteen years, right out of college, to the second guy she ever dated. She's not so much having a midlife crisis (for one thing, she's too young) as she is a midlife explosion.

"It's the first time I've been free since I was twenty-two, and I'm a different person now. I'm enjoying every minute of it."

Guys don't know how to respond to a woman who doesn't call back, but who's calling all the shots.

"I think of it as my wall," says Paula. "I'm still reeling from the hurt of my marriage, so I'm only going in so far. I've been seeing someone for six months, and my friends still haven't met him. At work he's only known as 'date guy.' I'm not even using his name! All I can say is that's where I'm at right now—I'll only get close to a certain point."

> "That's where I'm at right now— I'll only get close to a certain point."

So let's say you're happy, you're healthy, you feel good, you have a great haircut, and you have a night or two to yourself—and you'd like to spend it engaged in adult activities. I don't think there is a hard-and-fast rule for how long you wait to have sex with a guy, if it's just sex you're looking for. My best advice for this (and I repeat it often) is: Don't do anything too stupid.

Protect Yourself

Now, there are other books and magazine articles and Web sites that have more and better information about this subject than I am going to go into here, but you should be aware of a few basic facts: STDs are on the rise, genital herpes is showing up where only oral herpes used to be, and weirdos, stalkers, and just plain bad guys are certainly out there. So no matter what you think your intentions are, when you are in the midst of something hot and steamy, something cold and latex-y doesn't always come up. It should.

Believe it or not, young people are much better trained in this line of thinking than my generation and those on either side of me—generations who fondly remember the halcyon free-love days and a time when AIDS and HIV did not exist. Even my doctor, who was a post-divorce dater herself (now remarried), admitted to me that while she advocates the safety of using a condom during oral sex, she really can't imagine it.

I'm simply saying that if casual sex is in your future—or present—you need to buy your own stash of condoms and get comfortable bringing them up and putting them on (him). Your date, no matter how much he visualized getting naked with you tonight while he was shaving and trimming and deodorizing, cannot be counted on to have even one Trojan in his wallet.

The other tip I have in addition to Don't Do Anything Too Stupid is that your place is off-limits with a guy you recently met online or whom you only know from one night out. I don't care if no one is home, I don't care if you live next to the president of the neighborhood crime watch—your home is off-limits. There is always a La Quinta, right? That way, if you change your mind, you leave. If he gets weird, at least he doesn't know where you live. And of course, if we're worried about all this we shouldn't be having sex with him in the first place. I know all this. *You* know all this. But sometimes making out in the corner of the bar all night leads to decisions you never thought you'd make.

Who Benefits from Friends-with-Benefits?

Now, if you're ready to get naked but you're not ready for a full-fledged relationship—and let's say the whole one-night-stand thing just isn't for you—then you may be considering hooking up with one of your male friends. This is known in the dating world as an FWB, or friends-with-benefits. A friends-with-benefits relationship basically means that two people like each other (that's the friends part) and are sleeping together (that's the benefits part). It's typically a no-strings-attached, non-exclusive arrangement where condom use and respect are paramount. There are a lot of different ways that partners set this up. Some FWBs date other people but don't talk about it. Some are completely open about anyone else they're seeing and talk about it to death. Some FWBs go out in public, some just stay indoors. It's really whatever the FWBs agree to. From what I know, it takes a lot of trust, honesty, and maturity. That's more than what some people bring to a "real" relationship.

> An FWB takes a lot of trust, honesty, and maturity. That's more than what some people bring to a "real" relationship.

One of my girlfriends has been seeing someone for about six months in an FWB relationship. They get together a couple of nights a week, have a glass of wine and nice conversation, and then they have great sex for the rest of the night.

This arrangement works for them because she considers him a true friend; they talk on the phone, they help each other out with work and home projects, she even took care of him when he had food poisoning, and if that's not friendship I don't know what is.

But now, she tells me, they never do anything together outside of the bedroom like they did in the beginning; they just do the great-sex part. Also, he has never introduced her to any of his friends. She said she is starting to feel like a scorned mistress, and that's making her feel bad. So she asked me if I thought she should keep dating him.

Well, first of all, you have to actually *be* dating someone to *keep* dating him. And that means you have to actually go on dates with him, which clearly my friend is not. So the answer to her question is, *Whaaat?*

Now, I have nothing against a friends-with-benefits relationship, as long as both people are collecting the benefits. It didn't sound as if my friend still was. Or maybe after all this time she just wanted more. Not everyone can sustain an intimate physical relationship without getting involved emotionally, too.

But trading up from no-strings-attached-sex to actually dating can be pretty tricky, especially if only one person

> Not everyone can sustain an intimate physical relationship without getting involved emotionally, too.

is driving the change. For example, my friend wants to change the setup and venue, as well as the dress code. Instead of just coming over and getting naked, now her FWB friend is expected to get dressed, stay dressed, go to dinner or the movies or whatever, while all the time what he really wants to do is to go back to her place and have great sex. When a guy does all that other stuff, it's even more than dating. It's called a *relationship.*

While an FWB is not the same as dating, I think it should have to pass the same test as all dating situations: If it doesn't feel right, don't do it. If you are feeling used, abused, excluded, mistreated, or simply ignored, annoyed, or pissed off, wean yourself from the great sex and end it. I know giving him up may be hard, but a "real" relationship *and* great sex are not mutually exclusive. (Yes, I mean with the same guy.)

Still, if you're not quite ready for the complexity of a boyfriend, but the FWB isn't doing it for you, I know something that will: the Rabbit. And for that you don't even have to shave your legs.

Beware the Lens of Your Libido

So how many dates until you have sex? If you are only looking for a hookup or casual sex, I guess the answer is half a date. That's if the chemistry clicks and you're both looking—or not looking—for the same thing, and you know you can handle it. Meaning you can handle it even if it's the best sex you've ever had and he never calls you again. Ever.

However, if you are looking for a relationship with the guy you are considering having sex with, my recommendation is to take it slow. I'll tell you why. When you have sex with someone whom you don't really know but you definitely like and want to know better, you will see everything about him through the lens of your libido. You will attribute qualities to him that he may or may not possess (you can't know if he has these qualities because you don't really know him yet), but you will assume he has them because you have a great time in bed.

Not only will you presume he has these wonderful qualities, but you may also turn a blind eye to traits he has that you don't really like—also because the sex is great, or maybe because you're just so damn happy to be in a relationship with someone, regardless of the terms.

If great sex was all you were looking for—fine. But we started this half of the conversation talking about how long to wait to have sex if you want something more than a fling. I don't think there's a hard rule here, either; I just think that if you sleep with a man right away, you will delay really getting to know who he is because you are so enjoying having sex with him.

And at some point you will learn that he isn't everything you've imagined him to be.

I have had long-term relationships that began with a first date that lasted more than twenty-four hours. Eventually, you start to find out things that *do* matter to you in a partner: Does he believe in God, for example? Does he have a good work ethic? How does he treat his dog, his friends, the barista at Starbucks?

Does he have road rage? Does he hate his mother? Does he *live* with his mother? Is he a slob? Does he cheat at golf?

These are character qualities that you just won't learn unless you get out from under the covers once in a while. And if you started out in bed, it may take you months to learn. By then, you could be fairly invested in the guy. You may be heavily in lust, you may have introduced him to your friends, you may have brought him to the office party. You may even think it's love. And it will be harder to untangle yourself from all this than if you had learned some of these things while your clothes were still on.

> Eventually, you start to find out things that *do* matter to you in a partner.

My guess is that soon you will not feel good about yourself or him if you continue to forgive his propensity for yelling at clerks or peeking at your text messages or borrowing money just because he's good in bed.

Your Brain on Love

And all the advice I just gave you? That's pretty much straight from my therapist, and it only cost you a few minutes and less than twenty dollars. You have no idea what a bargain that is. Of course, you don't have to come back next week and tell me *how's that working for you?*

I have come up with a personal solution to this, however. From now on, any potential boyfriends are going to have to date my therapist before they date me. Because when I'm falling in lust or love or even like-you-a-lot, it's like being on mind-altering drugs. Something equivalent to say, several Cosmos or the best stuff you smoked in college. It's enough to send my senses reeling—all five of them, and that's completely excluding my common sense.

According to the experts who study loveology, when we talk about "feeling chemistry" after meeting Mr. Right we are dead-on accurate. Falling in love wreaks havoc with your brain's chemicals, causing great surges in dopamine, adrenaline, and endorphins. These are the culprits responsible for spine-tingling feelings like ecstasy, bliss, rapture. They are also freakishly similar biochemically to obsessive-compulsive disorder. So when you've got the hots for someone, it's like you've suddenly contracted an amped-up case of OCD.

> **When I'm falling in lust or love or even like-you-a-lot, it's like being on mind-altering drugs.**

Just think how many times you, your best friend, your sister, or your co-worker has said: "I think I'm in love with [insert name of date du jour] and I can't stop thinking about him." Enough said.

This is your brain. This is your brain on love.

So given the fact that I have been known to get loopy on just two Advil, how can I possibly make a wise decision about whom to date when all these chemicals are making me higher than those pot-smoking kids on the Anti-Drug commercials who sit around watching TV all day? If I am completely without my senses, I shouldn't even be *driving* to see my therapist.

Is there a Breathalyzer test for the love-doped?

Officer: "Excuse me, ma'am, I have been following you for three miles with my lights flashing and my siren blaring. Not only did you not respond, you ran two red lights, knocked over a pedestrian's shopping cart, and your car muffler is trailing toilet paper. Step out of the car and tell me what kind of drugs you're on."

Me: "Oh, Officer, I am so sorry. I assure you I am completely sober. It's just that I met this cute guy and we spent the last hour gazing into each other's eyes at this little lunch place in midtown. I can't stop thinking about him and my mind is obsessed with wedding details. Can you just give me a warning?"

Rather than risk Atlanta's Finest pulling me over, my date will just have to drive himself. To his appointment. To see my therapist.

Don't worry, she's very cool, very wise, and doesn't do any of that *tell me about your mother* stuff. I should know. I've been seeing her for fifteen years.

I know what you're thinking—I'm a lifer. Maybe I am. But I can tell you with absolute assurance that my marriage would have ended with one of us in jail for resenting the other one to death had it not been for Amanda, licensed therapist. That I might not have known when it was okay to finally stop trying and let it go. That we would not have the extraordinary divorce and friendship we have today had it not been for what my ex and I learned in therapy.

It's just that we met Amanda one year too late.

I wonder how things would have been if I had sent my ex-husband to Amanda when he was still just my boyfriend. Say, for an evaluation—*before* I committed to love, honor, and cherish him forever, no matter what. Forever is a freakin' long time. And *no matter what* is a phrase that just doesn't belong anywhere near a committed relationship. But you're not thinking about that under the chuppa because your senses are still reeling from the pathology of love pulsing through your veins. And standing so close to him . . . well, don't even get me started on pheromones.

So, I'm thinking my therapist can give me kind of a rate card for my next boyfriend. Something simple like . . .

- On a scale of one to five, how heavy is his baggage (and can he carry it himself)? Does it match or clash with mine?

- On a scale of one to five, how likely is he to sleep with my best friend? His best friend?

- On a scale of one to five, how likely are his cute little idiosyncrasies (calling me five times a day just to say hello) to drive me certifiably crazy before "forever" is even halfway up?

- Or how about something simple, like: On a scale of one to five, how likely are we to have a lifelong love?

With this psychological report card from my therapist, I would now be armed with a powerful antidote to the drugs taking over my mind, body, and heart. When the surge of hormones surges, I can whip out the rate card and try to put some logic around the illogical process of falling in love. Perhaps I can actually catch myself *before* I fall.

Yeah, I'm smirking over that last line, too.

Who among us has ever walked away from a potentially disastrous match because someone told us that he was wrong for us? Come on. Show of hands. I thought not.

> Who among us has ever walked away from a potentially disastrous match because someone told us that he was wrong for us?

How many people whose opinion I trusted told me I should stop and reconsider marrying my ex? Or at least slow down?

Well, let's start with the woman who introduced us—the lead singer in his band and a really good friend of mine. She didn't actually introduce us as in, "I think you two would make a great couple." She hired me to do the band's press kit, and I met him over interviews. In fact, she actually warned me from day one that this was not going to work, and she had valid reasons—proof—as well as a background in mental health for crying out loud. Did I listen? Uh, yeah, that's a rhetorical question.

Next, my best friend of fifteen years, in her sweet, tender way, said to me when she met him, "This isn't the guy you were telling me about, is it?" And when she looked at me expectantly, I could hear her thought mantra: *Sayitisn'tso-sayitisn'tso-sayitisn'tso.*

So what makes me think I would listen to the impartial evaluation of my therapist? What makes me think anything she said could have stopped the love train I was on? I mean, thirty minutes after we told my parents that we were engaged, my mom was looking at bridesmaid dresses. You think I'm kidding? I wish I had tested the dopamine levels in *her* brain when she learned her youngest daughter was getting married—finally.

I'm betting that no one could have talked me out of marrying my ex. I was truly in love and thought I had complete control of my senses. And truth be told, I don't regret having married him. We have the miracle of our son (and I mean miracle), and my ex is one of my best friends. He is the ideal man for me . . . to be in a divorce with.

Still, if someone really wants to date me, he probably should keep that appointment with my therapist. Maybe he can convince her to open my files and the two of them can spend some time delving into the question of am *I* right for *him?* I just hope he asks how big a trunk he'll need for my baggage.

Chapter 13

Love, Lies, and Loans

The biggest complaint women have about dating—online or oth-erwise—is that men are not who they say they are. Of course, if friends fix you up with someone they know, they can pretty much fill you in on the guy's family and marital status, occupation, even some personality traits. But even they can't tell you how he treats a woman—unless, of course, he is the ex of the friend who is fix-ing you up. And that begs the question, *Why is he your ex?* I would definitely ask this. And not rhetorically. Get an answer!

While people can be deceptive face-to-face, online dating sites make it even easier for people to misrepresent themselves. You probably won't know until it's too late.

Nancy told me she started e-mailing with a guy from Match who said he had a master's in computers. Well, so does she. She asked him a few light questions and reported that from his responses there was no way he did technology for a living. Why would a person lie about that? Because he *can.*

Picture This

The first red flag in dating online would be no picture on the profile. "He's either married or he's ugly," says Nancy. Of course, he could just not have gotten around to it yet. If you see a profile that you like, ask for the photo—one time. Ask him to post it or send it to you via the site—never to your personal e-mail address. If you get a lot of pushback or a picture that looks like a magazine model, or if he says he doesn't have any pictures or doesn't know how to upload one (if you can do it, so can he), then move on. Everyone should be able to show a photo—everyone who is upfront and single, that is.

Now, the reverse is not necessarily true. Some married men do have their photos posted on their online profile. I guess they just assume that no one they know is on the site, and plenty of women who don't know any better are. So, if you end up dating one of these guys, here are a couple of clues:

- He can never go out on a weekend night.

- You never go out with any of his friends.

- He avoids going out with your friends.

- After six months of dating, he never invites you to his home. If he tells you this is because the last girl he dated went psycho on him and came to his house at all hours of the night so he doesn't invite anyone over anymore, that is probably a line. Do I sound bitter about this? That's because that was the line a guy used on me. And I was too dumb or too much in denial to figure it out until much later.

Now let's say you've been dating a guy for a long time and you think you know him well, but he does some of these things and he doesn't have a good explanation for them. What do you do? (Everybody now): Move on! When someone is taking us for a ride, we often can't believe it . . . or don't want to believe it. Believe it. It happens. Trust your intuition, not the lies.

> **When someone is taking us for a ride, we often can't believe it . . . or don't want to believe it. Believe it.**

Other possible clues that the guy you're dating is married:

- If he lives out of town and just calls you when he's in town. Tell him you want his address; that you'd like to send flowers, chocolates, or a private detective.

- If he only calls you or texts you from a cell phone. I know that many people don't have landlines anymore, but you should get an e-mail once in a while from his work address, at the very least.

- If he can only see you during the week or at lunchtime.

- If he has a fortieth birthday party and doesn't invite you. (Yes, me again.)

- If he never introduces you to his family.

- If he can never spend the night.

The Internet has made it easier than ever for married men to meet unsuspecting women. And listen, married men are great dates. They often lavish you with praise, gifts, attention. You are a desirable distraction from their otherwise tormented (or just bored) lives. That's not what you want, trust me. I am sorry for all the ones who may hit on you, take you out, fall in love with you and vice versa. Look for the signs and save yourself some deep hurt.

Another red flag are those guys who say they love you after the first couple of dates. If a guy has "fallen in love" with me this fast, he has fallen in love with his idea of who I am. He can't possibly love me, because he doesn't even know me.

"I can almost hear some guys sitting across from me going, *Hair, good. Teeth, good. I think I could marry this girl,*" says Bonnie. "I was with this one guy who declared his love after the second date. When I told him I was nowhere near where he was on the love scale, he asked me if I thought I could maybe catch up with him. Uh, no."

> If a guy has "fallen in love" with me this fast, he has fallen in love with his idea of who I am.

Sex and Lies

Some men are really good at compartmentalizing their lives. They are so good at lying that they truly believe what they say. Do you remember the episode of *Seinfeld* when Jerry has to take a lie detector test? He's really nervous, until he talks to his best friend George.

George tells him, "Remember, Jerry, it's not a lie . . . if you believe it."

I think I've met a few guys who are like this—it's scary! They can be hard to spot because they are usually good looking, charming, and very, very good at not telling the truth. Not even to themselves. But eventually you will catch him in a lie, or several. Now it's up to you—do you want to live in denial and be deceived? It really is a choice; maybe you're okay with not knowing the other half of his life. But if something about his life, his lines, his love doesn't add up, ask him about it. Someone who is not lying will be able to make sense. On the other hand, a liar will likely get defensive, angry, and accusatory with you. This makes *you* feel like the bad guy—he'll be hurt that you don't trust him. And you may really feel bad. That's what he wants. It takes the spotlight off him, and believe me, he was hot under there. Anyone who has nothing to hide should be willing to talk about whatever is bothering you. You should not feel bad for asking; you should not feel wrong if you still don't believe him. You should protect yourself and your feelings.

And remember, if you are intimate with someone who is lying to you, you are putting more than your heart at risk. You are risking your sexual health, because you have no idea who else he is sleeping with . . . and lying to.

Little Old Ladies Aren't the Only Ones

How many women do you know who have loaned money to their boyfriend? To their boyfriend of less than six months? Six *weeks*?

Now how many do you know who have been paid back? I don't know why women do this—well, yes I do. To help. To save. To avoid being lonely. But if anyone you meet—online or off—asks you for a loan, to invest in a "sure winner," or to co-sign a lease or a bank loan, there is only one thing to say: No. Say it sweetly. Say it nicely. But say it firmly and mean it. If he pressures you the next day or next week, I'm sorry to say, he wants more than your love.

There are plenty of scams and scammers out there; online dating just gives them another point of entry. There are so many worthy causes that could use your money—don't give it away to someone who's willing to break your heart and ruin your credit rating.

> There is only one thing to say: No. Say it sweetly. Say it nicely. But say it firmly and mean it.

Men who are married, men who are scammers, men who are not completely forthcoming do have one thing going for them that some of us women just can't resist: They create drama. We all know that some women love the roller-coaster ride, right up until the moment we have to throw up. If you've been in relationships like this, you know there always comes a time when you want to flag down the operator and beg him to let you off.

Girlfriend, it's time to leave the carnival altogether. Sooner or later (and damn if it isn't always later than we'd hope) drama becomes a drag.

The addict or alcoholic who needs you so much he will take everything you have to give and still require more? He won't be there when you need him—heck, he's not there when he needs himself. The abusive man who's so remorseful and repentant after he's put you down or pushed you up against a wall? He is not worth your broken heart or broken bones. He will cause wounds deeper than those you can see on the surface.

Do these men deserve our friendship, help, and support? Maybe. If they are getting help and support for themselves, definitely maybe. All I'm saying is that these types of personalities should be in your non-negotiables under "things to avoid . . . again," and maybe you should pin that to your collar and tape it to your mirror and stick it on your dashboard (you can't even see my dashboard anymore for all the Post-it notes). It's time to break your dating patterns if you've always picked up strays or bad boys or victims or anyone who needs to be saved more than he needs a relationship. Wean yourself and try a nice, normal guy. You may not think he'll leave you breathless (although I bet he will if you let him), but he won't leave you bankrupt or bruised, either. And dating guys without so much heartache will actually give you a chance to see what a healthy relationship is like . . . there's a lot to learn and love when you're not the one always coming to the rescue.

The best defense against what to avoid is your own self-respect. Get some. Get some more. And never again take anything from anyone that goes against who you are, what you believe in, and what you deserve.

And when you miss the drama? Call me. We'll go to the movies.

Chapter 14

The New World of Dating

SOMETIMES I IMAGINE MYSELF AS AN ALIEN WHO HAS JUST discovered that there is human life on Earth and has come to visit. I swoop down into a major city (such as the one I live in) and have a look around. I check out the billboards and notice that the women here all seem to want bigger breasts, flatter stomachs, smaller hips, and a poisonous substance injected between their eyebrows. I would see that the men want larger penises, a fast vasectomy, and to go to a place called Hooters where the women seem to have done the bigger-breasts thing.

I would see people driving or walking or skateboarding, holding a little black (or pink or silver) flat rectangular object, and they would be rapidly moving their thumbs over the keys and reading small text in a small window. Or some would be holding the flat black thing up to their faces and yelling intimate details of their lives. Other people would have a blue flashing light on top of their ear and appear to be talking—also loudly—into the air. (Unlike my human form, I would naturally be attracted to these blue-flashing-light people, being an alien and all.)

There would be long lines of people ordering $4 cups of something called a vanilla-latte-fat-free-soy-hold-the-whip and sitting nearby typing on larger black or silver rectangles—this time using most of their fingers and none of their thumbs.

And when I picked up the local paper and turned to the back page, I would see that this city was filled with unusual mating rituals. There would be pictures of blond women and sculpted men asking me to come to Lock and Key parties, GamePlay parties, or to Just Do Lunch! I'd see ads for swinger parties and speed dating. And everyone would be online, apparently waiting to have sex with me *tonight*.

Isn't this what we in the post-divorce-dating world are bombarded with on a daily basis? How in the world do you know which dating rituals to try? Well, I went on a few playdates in the past two years, and I'm here to give you the highlights. Then you can decide what's worth your valuable dating time and what's not.

Lock and Key Parties

This sounded like a blast to me. But when I mention Lock and Key parties to people, they think it's one of those parties where the women throw their house keys in a bowl and the men each pick one. It's *not*. I've never been to one of those parties, and I can't say the blind-taste-test approach appeals to me, unless the guy who picks my keys happens to be a housepainter running a special.

No, a Lock and Key party is a dating gimmick that gives new meaning to the word *icebreaker*. Each guy gets a key and each woman gets a lock and you're supposed to find the person whose key fits your lock. No sexual undertones there, huh?

The first Lock and Key party I went to was held at a hip new club north of the city. I walked in and paid my $20 to the guy host, who had about twenty-five chains around his neck. On each chain was a lock. These were no itty-bitty-charm locks; these were real, solid brass Schlage models. The chains with the locks on them are what the women wear, and let me tell you, when he put one over my neck, it was heavy.

> Each guy gets a key and each woman gets a lock and you're supposed to find the person whose key fits your lock.

Next to the guy with the locks was the female hostess, with a bunch of chains around her neck, each holding the keys to all the locks. These are the necklaces the guys wear. Is there a ball-and-chain joke here somewhere?

The place was packed, music was playing but not blaring, colored lights washed the walls. Fun, I thought. There were about seventy-five people standing around the bar, and next to the dance floor was a table set up with more lock and key necklaces, a roll of bright orange tickets, and what could only be door prizes.

I went up to the bar, lurching a little from the weight of the lock dangling between my breasts, and ordered a drink. Before I could turn around, four or five men were literally circling me, waiting to see if their key fit my lock.

Now, this is where the concept breaks down a little. It's not as if these men said, "Hey, who's the beautiful redhead who just walked in?" and then lined up to meet me. It was more like, "Hey, there's a lock I haven't tried. Let's see if my key fits."

> **Before I could turn around, four or five men were literally circling me, waiting to see if their key fit my lock.**

And why was this so important to the men? Because in addition to icebreaking and meeting people whom you'd potentially like to see again—preferably without a lock or key around their neck—there's another layer to the party: Each time a guy's key fits your lock, both of you get to go up to the table, get a bright orange ticket, and obtain a new lock and key so you can keep meeting other people and trying their locks. The tickets are for chances to win door prizes. The more tickets you get, the greater your chances of winning a door prize.

Well, men are nothing if not goal-oriented. So what I saw taking place would have been funny if it wasn't just so . . . *guy.*

A man would walk up to a woman and ask to see if his key fit. (Good so far.) But if the guy's key did not fit, *he would walk away.* Presumably to try someone else's lock. I saw this happen five times in five minutes! Uh, hello? Why have an icebreaker if you're not going to stick around to

> **Men are nothing if not goal-oriented.**

see if you can make it melt? So *what* if your key doesn't fit—you have approached an attractive woman with a great smile and nice legs and all you care about is whether or not your key fits? How about some banter? How about a drink? How about "to hell with the key—what's your name?"

Instead, men (and some women) were making a mad dash around the bar, fiddling with locks and keys and shrieking when one fit, then running to the door prize table for a ticket and another necklace so they could keep playing.

I couldn't just stand by and watch (and laughing wasn't making me very popular), so I asked someone about this. I watched a cute guy get up the nerve to walk up to a pretty girl, try her lock, then walk away when it didn't fit. I ran up to him (yes, me being ladylike again, running in heels in a bar) and said, "Excuse me, I just have to ask you . . . I saw you staring at that girl for, like, ten minutes. Why did you walk away when you finally met her?"

"My key didn't fit," he said, with the unspoken *duh* hanging in the air.

"Hmmm," I said, ever so gently, "I think the key thing is just a way to make it easy to meet someone . . . say hello . . . see what happens . . . you know?"

"But everyone is trying to unlock the most locks, get the most tickets . . . ," he said lamely.

"Yeah," I said, "to win a friggin' hair dryer!"

Pause. Beat. Two. Three . . .

He literally slapped himself on the head. Then he ripped off his necklace and headed back to the girl. Midway there, he stopped, turned around, and walked back toward me with an apologetic smile.

"Uh, mind if I try *your* lock first?"

That caveman mentality is hard to break. But I'm working on it.

My take on the Lock and Key party is that it's definitely fun and easy to meet people. You'll feel perfectly comfortable going alone because the key thing really is a good icebreaker. You'll be talking to guys in no time if you can get them to see beyond the door prize draw.

Just as in dating, we all run the risk of getting caught up in quantity, the number of locks we open, and what kinds of keys fit. And while I think it's true that you have to meet a lot of people to find a potential or two, it's not all about the game.

After all, some of the guys trying to win the hair dryer didn't even have hair.

Speed Dating

Most of the women I talk to say that when they are on a date, they can "tell" within the first ten minutes.

Tell what?

Tell if the guy's a jerk. Tell if there's chemistry. Tell if they will go out with him again or not. Yes, all this in ten minutes.

Do I hear six minutes? Because six minutes is how long you get to meet, greet, and repeat when you're speed dating. During a typical speed dating event, you can run through twenty guys in two hours. At what other time could you say, "So many men, so little time," and literally mean it?

I was wary of speed dating, because it sounded an awful lot like quickie interviews, and I'm not into interviews (or quickies, for that matter). But after my first speed dating event, I highly recommend it to anyone who has a presentable appearance (you don't have to look like a celebrity) and can hold a reasonably engaging conversation.

The first reason I like speed dating is that I believe six minutes really is the perfect amount of time for a first date. Just about the time I'm ready to yawn, move on, or say something stupid because I like the guy, a bell rings and he's gone. I wish this happened in every area of my life. Just think of all the messy situations I could have avoided with my family, my ex, my bosses.

> Six minutes really is the perfect amount of time for a first date.

Speed dating is a lot like musical chairs, except instead of music you get conversation—sometimes inane, sometimes brilliant, always entertaining.

You have to register for a speed dating party ahead of time, because there are a few details that the organizers have to get just right. First, there is usually an age group—twenty-five- to thirty-five-year-olds; thirty-five to forty-five; forty-five to fifty-five; and so on. This way, older women aren't competing with pretty young things and young hot guys aren't competing with older, richer guys. And vice versa for all that. There were no specialty groups for cougars and their prey, or MILFs and those who would LF them, which kind of bummed me out, but I sucked it up and went to the speed dating party for my actual age group.

Detail two: The event coordinators have to manage the sign-up process so that there are equal numbers of guys and girls. That's because the party is basically divided up into six-minute rounds; if there aren't enough women for the men, for example, then the men have to sit a round or two out, and that does not make them very happy by the time they get to you. No one pays forty bucks to get a bye.

When I went online to sign up for my speed dating party, I was told there were no spaces left for women. However, if I was able to find a guy to sign up, I could go.

I convinced my ex-husband to go with me.

I think it may cost me my child support.

The party was at a trendy bar downtown, and we arrived at 8:00 p.m. on a Friday night—long before real people go to the bars downtown. The speed daters were the only people in the place. Everyone was given a clipboard and a list of first-names-only of the people we would meet that night. Each person was also assigned a number. There were spaces on the sheet for us to add notes, and a column for us to check "Yes" or "No." At the end of the night, if you and another person (presumably of the opposite sex) checked Yes next to each other's name, you would receive his e-mail address and he would receive yours the next day.

How hard could this be?

The night I went, the women were each given one spot to sit in all night long while the guys revolved around us. And that's exactly how it should be, right?

I was shown to a beautiful small room off to the right of the bar—it had a fireplace, low lighting (the kind in which I look best), and a long couch. In front of the couch were three coffee tables spaced to create three separate "date areas," and each table had a tent card on it with the number four, five, or six. I put on my name/number tag: I was number five for the female team. Females number four and six were supposed to be seated on either side of me. Since there were no other chairs, I assumed the men would sit next to each of us on the couch when it was their turn.

The rest of the females were seated along the bar and in two other small rooms that were much like the one I was in. As I settled onto the couch, the men were given a starting number corresponding to the woman they were supposed to meet first, and a list of who to see during each round throughout the night.

This particular speed dating party had signed up eleven men and eleven women. At eight o'clock, I noticed that the seats on either side of me were still empty; I had the room to myself. I was considering whether or not this was a good thing when the first-round bell rang. My six minutes were about to start; I couldn't waste time thinking about the female no-shows. My job was to date—fast.

I positioned myself in the middle of the couch behind table number five, adjusted my top to make sure not too much was showing, and greeted my first speed dater with a big smile. Before I could shake his hand he began talking—well, spewing, to be more accurate. He gave me five minutes' worth of information in sixty seconds. Since this was my first speed date, I suddenly became worried that I wasn't sent all the rules—were we *supposed* to talk as if we were the auctioneer at a foreclosure?

In one breath my first man of the night said: "Hi, I'm Michael I'm a software developer I work in Buckhead but I live in Marietta the drive's not too bad really I ride bikes for fun I don't have kids but I love them I'm a Virgo I graduated from Georgia Tech where my brother also went but we didn't live together because he's sort of a slob and I'm neat but not obsessive I've been divorced two years and I don't have any children but I'd like to someday oh I already said that. Is this your first time speed dating?"

And with that he took a huge breath and stopped, waiting for me to answer.

As I subtly wiped the spittle off my face and chest, I tried to process what he'd said since there were no obvious pauses that allowed me to get my head around things like the traffic and when is Virgo's birthday anyway?

Noticing my confused look and my inability to speak, Michael said, speaking only slightly slower, "You *are* number five, aren't you? It's says so on your name tag and the table so of course you are and well on my sheet I'm supposed to see you first."

I touched my name tag and the room stopped spinning—I was only drinking club soda but the way he talked made me feel like someone had slipped me something.

> "This is my first time speed dating and I didn't realize it was going to be so . . . speedy."

"I'm sorry," I said, very slowly. "Uh, this is my first time speed dating and I didn't realize it was going to be so . . . speedy."

He laughed a little then stopped abruptly and said, "Well, this is my fourth time and I've learned to try to get as much in as possible right upfront because the time goes by really fast."

He was bouncing his knees up and down like a nervous kid waiting outside the principal's office, and I got the feeling that his normal speaking mannerisms weren't much different from those of his speed-dating self.

"So what do you do?" he asked me, and as I started to say "I'm a wri—" he interrupted me and asked, "Are you from Atlanta?"

"Uh, no," I said, and then went to finish the word "writer" when he said, "Do you have kids?"

I didn't think he would let me speak so I simply held up one finger as he pounced. "Boy or girl?" I pointed to Michael's pants to indicate "boy" and, anticipating his next question, I got a jump on him and said, "Eleven!" Somehow I felt as if I'd just scored one point.

Undaunted, Michael continued telling me things about himself as if he were speed-reading from a personals ad. "I love traveling, reading autobiographies, listening to music, and long walks on the beach. Did you ever live near the beach?"

"I grew up in Florida," I managed to say before he launched into a story about his childhood in Wilmington, North Carolina. I think he was just getting to middle school when—thankfully— the bell rang.

Michael bounded up and asked me where number four was—his next date. I looked to my right and my left and noticed that both spaces were still empty. I shrugged (I'd given up talking a good two minutes ago) and he stomped his foot, glaring at me as if it were somehow my fault. The party organizer—having seen the foot stomping—came into the room and explained that Michael would be sitting this round out and could she buy him a drink? He did not look happy but he took his stomping with him to the bar.

End of Round One.

I marked a huge "X" through Michael's name.

I had higher hopes for Round Two.

I shouldn't have.

William came in, shook my hand, and read my name tag.

"Your name is Ginger, huh?" he asked, stating the very obvious. "Where's Gilligan?" and with that he started laughing. Not just laughing, shrieking. Snorting. Guffawing. Really, he guffawed.

> **With that he started laughing. Not just laughing, shrieking. Snorting. Guffawing.**

It took all my willpower not to say what I typically say to guys who use this Gilligan line on me, and who have used this Gilligan line on me for the past thirty-three years, which is, *Funny. Never heard that one before.*

I didn't say this because I had every confidence in myself that I could refrain from severe sarcasm for six minutes. Plus I had paid to be here.

Then he looked at me. Well, he looked at my hair. Closely.

"You have red hair?" he asked.

"Yes, I do—it's kind of hard to see in this light, I guess."

"Are you a *real* redhead?" he asked, looking me down and up, and drawing out the word *reeaaal.*

I was insulted by the demeaning question, but I told myself I had nine more men to go and I couldn't have them locking me in my room for bad behavior. I thought I had it under control when my mouth suddenly got a brain of its own and said, "No, I'm really a blonde, so I don't understand the sleazy innuendo of your question but it doesn't matter because oh, wow, did you just hear the bell? Time's up."

End of Round Two.

Some other opening lines included:

"You're not here for anything serious, right? Because I'm totally not, so, uh, don't get your hopes up."

Don't worry.

RING!

"Can you fucking believe four women did not show up? That sucks, doesn't it? Fuck. If I find out who they are I'm going to fuckin' go off on them."

RING!

"Hi, do you mind if I just skip you and go to number eight? She's so hot. I've scoped everyone else out and I think if I play it right and get to her early I can get, like, ten extra minutes."

> "Hi, do you mind if I just skip you and go to number eight? She's so hot."

RING!

Most of the men were actually very personable and ranged from somewhat attractive to pretty good looking. None was downright ugly—in speech or in manner. One guy was pretty drunk, but he was British so I think he thought that was a good cover. It wasn't. (I wouldn't recommend drinking while you speed date because you sit so close to each other to talk that the smell of alcohol really is pretty obnoxious, even if you aren't.)

I liked Chris, a high school history teacher, well enough to mark "Yes" next to his name, even though he was really into Civil War reenactments and seemed to know every make and model of war weaponry. But he was very open about wanting to find a meaningful relationship, and how difficult it could be while raising three sons. He scored big for intelligence and sincerity. And he's going to need to know that war strategy when his sons reach high school.

I liked Craig, who seemed to have worked up a short stand-up comic routine. As most women will swear, a sense of humor—especially with a dose of wit—will get a man further than wine and roses. I'm a big believer that laughing is the ultimate aphrodisiac.

I liked Charles, who was a banker and seemed very down-to-earth. We did get in a bit of a heated discussion about the mortgage crisis but he was a gentleman and never once raised his voice or threatened to hit me with his *Wall Street Journal*. He even said those rarely spoken words that every woman loves to hear from a man: "You may be right." Now, that is one smart guy.

Maybe I just liked the guys whose names started with *C*?

These were all guys who had either been married or close to it and weren't either anymore. They had jobs, they had friends, they had families, they had teeth, and, just like me, they had hopes for finding a relationship again. Most of them had done speed dating before and liked meeting a lot of women quickly and in person (as opposed to online dating, which most of them also did. Do). The men (and women) said that speed dating works because most of us won't date people we are not physically attracted to, and that's something you can definitely tell in six minutes. So it is, in fact, fast.

You also get a quick sense of other compatible areas—personality, intelligence, humor, lifestyle, manners—at least enough to know whether or not you would see him again for another date. Maybe twelve minutes next time.

When it was time for my ex's round, he came in, plopped on my couch (I had begun to think of the couch and fireplace as my room, since the other women never showed up), and said, "I was going to leave after round two because rounds three and four were no-shows and nobody here really seems like my type. Except the bartender. And she won't talk to me. I think it's against the rules."

I said, "So if you didn't know me and hadn't already married and divorced me, you would think I was the hottest chick here?"

"Oh, yeah," he said. "By far. Have you *seen* the women here?"

Not exactly the compliment I thought it was going to be.

"Hey," he said, "we should start making out. That would get them talking."

But we didn't. Instead we talked about the upcoming weekend and who would be taking our son where.

"I'm glad we had this time to catch up for eighty bucks," my ex said, and we started laughing. We were still laughing when the bell rang and my next date came in.

"Oh," he said, "you two look as if you're having a great time. Good for you. I'll just give you some more time."

And with that we started laughing even harder.

We turned in our clipboards at the end of the night. My ex had not circled any of the women. I had circled a couple of the guys I liked, and put a star next to one I thought was really cute.

Someone told me later that he was gay.

I had no idea. I guess that takes more than six minutes to figure out.

Chapter 15

Dating More than One Person at a Time

(or How I Learned to Juggle Men)

AT ONE POINT I WAS SEEING THREE MEN AT ONCE (WELL, not all at one time, but you know what I mean). They all knew about one another and we were all respectful of each other's privacy and safety. To be clear, none of them was sitting home waiting for me on the nights that I was out with someone else. In fact, I found that it takes having several options just to find one guy who is free for a Saturday night. Everyone is really busy in the post-divorce-dating world—work, kids, searching online for their next ex.

This arrangement was perfect for me at the time, and I enjoyed the unique qualities of each man very much. That's one of the things I like most about dating. You are always going out and meeting new people and learning new stuff and hearing new stories. It's enough to make me a serial dater.

The first ball in the air—I'll call him Renaud—was an incredible gentleman with an alluring progressive streak. He was actually my age—unusual for me since I typically date younger men.

Sometimes much younger. I loved Renaud's brain and business savvy and the way he embraced life. Of course I loved the way he looked, too. Let's just get this out in the open: When you're dating, you should be dating people you are attracted to and who are attracted to you. No matter how much we love the beauty inside, you have to have chemistry. Of course, a lot of guys get better looking the more you know them. If a guy is brilliant and witty, or kind and thoughtful, or in great shape and has a great attitude (or all of the above), his personality can make him as striking as anything on the outside. I really mean that. But there has to be something that makes you to want to know him in the first place, right?

> **A lot of guys get better looking the more you know them.**

Renaud and I had a mutual understanding of a relationship that was casual but caring; open but respectful. We enjoyed going out, having dinner with friends, exploring anything interesting. From Renaud I learned how to date gracefully. He taught me that true gentlemen (and ladies) never kiss and tell. There should be no gossiping, no scorecards, no tally sheet.

Unless you're writing a book, of course.

I also learned from Renaud that even beautiful men look for more than physical beauty in their women. He once said that it was hard for him, at his age (late forties), to find the right combination of qualities in a woman. Younger women wanted to get married and have kids; older women wanted security. Since I wasn't looking for either, Renaud could be, do, say anything he liked, because nothing in our relationship depended on him being anything other than himself. I was independent, self-sufficient, laidback about our relationship but up for just about anything. He said that was attractive.

> Nothing in our relationship depended on him being anything other than himself.

I was surprised that one of the things I found really charming about Renaud was that he was a great father to his teenage children. Welcome to what's hot in post-divorce dating. Renaud took fathering very seriously and was a natural at it; we talked about our kids and he gave me great perspective about raising boys. Renaud didn't try to be Superdad and he recognized that he didn't always know the right thing to do. But he was a committed, loving primary parent, and I have to tell you, that was sexy.

Renaud and I dated casually for most of a year—not exclusively, but consistently. While we had chemistry and friendship, we didn't have what my friend Jennie calls the "it" factor. We're both dating other people now, but we're still friends. That's one of the great surprises about post-divorce dating: You get to add people to your life, and there aren't a lot of opportunities to do that when you're, say, over forty. It's not like we're in college and there's a steady stream of new people to meet each semester. Or people you meet again because you don't remember meeting

> That's one of the great surprises about post-divorce dating: You get to add people to your life.

them the first time due to the amount of grain alcohol being consumed.

Bachelor Number Two, we'll call him Evan, was a *much* younger man. When I mentioned how old he was to my good friend Lisa, she actually shrieked. It didn't bother me—except that I couldn't hear for a couple of hours. Lisa wasn't judging me; she didn't say she couldn't be friends with me anymore if I kept seeing Evan. She was just surprised. Shocked. Jealous.

Evan was bright and adorable and opinionated and fearless. He taught me that women could be sexy at any age, and that *sexy* does not depend on some Barbie-doll definition. One of our best dates was spent canoeing down the river. It was the first time since my divorce that I'd felt so physically strong—all those kick-boxing and Pilates classes do eventually pay off. Evan is a rare breed of man who actually likes to have conversations. His were the kind of deep talks you only seem to have when you're young and rebellious and think you know everything—before you get older and realize you don't really know much at all. I liked listening to him because his thoughts were creative and passionate. Plus, we weren't in a serious relationship so I didn't have to convince him of anything.

Dating younger men isn't for everyone; there is a bit of "me-versus-the-establishment" attitude. And, um, well, I *am* the establishment. You're also going to find that "home" means an apartment with an air mattress, cinder blocks for shelves, and sometimes something growing on a windowsill that looks remarkably like contraband. There are other differences . . . are you comfortable not making plans until the last minute because who knows when his buddy will call and want to play Xbox Live? (This is the same Xbox Live my son plays, by the way.) Do you really want to go out with his friends on beer-and-trivia night, whether he invites you or not? Call me immature, but I was fine with all this, most of the time.

There was a certain loneliness in my yearlong relationship with Evan. With our lives so different and separate, sometimes I felt like a secret obsession. There was also a sad realization in knowing that it would never be more than this, that it would never go further, regardless of how much fun it was. In addition to juggling men, I was juggling a lot of new emotions, too.

When I started dating someone else more seriously, Evan was the first person I had to learn to let go of in a long, long time. I am one of those people who hold on to people. I am still friends with almost every ex-boyfriend I ever had; I still hang out with friends I've known for twenty-five years. During my post-divorce dating, I learned that I couldn't hold on to everyone. Evan was the first.

> In addition to juggling men, I was juggling a lot of new emotions, too.

Then I met a man I liked more than anyone I had met yet. He fit a lot of my nice-to-haves (which, as you read in chapter 4, are different from non-negotiables and must-haves, of which he also had quite a few). Joel and I had met on Match.com and had gone through the getting-to-know-you progression, all the way up to talking on the phone for several months. So we knew each other but had never met in person. His home base was my city but he was working on assignment out west. When we finally did meet, one of those things happened that I tell my friends never happens: We had an instant connection. I loved his looks, his smile, his mind; he was funny, irreverent, caring, and he was holding a bouquet of flowers he had selected stem by stem himself—I don't know how he got away with this without seeming sappy. But there is nothing sappy about Joel. He is a total gentleman with a killer ladies'-man streak. What is it about us that we like a little bit of that bad-boy vibe? I was clearly in trouble.

Throwing another man into the mix—someone I wanted to be with more than anyone yet—rocked my precariously balanced dating world. Despite my intentions not to, I fell. Hard. But Joel lived out of town; he wanted a family someday (and I was past the stage of having more); he was still racking 'em up and knocking 'em dead; and for half a dozen other reasons that I can't even explain, it was over almost as soon as it began.

But Joel helped me see luminous things about love, life, and myself. He was an unguarded romantic, and he unabashedly adored me and let me know I inspired him. He was good-natured about my nurturing streak, and yet he was the first man I had met in a long time who appeared to be fully capable. He gave me hope that there was someone out there on whose shoulders I could rest my head and let him carry the world for a while. It just wasn't going to be Joel.

Joel helped my heart open up just the tiniest bit, but it was enough. He also promptly broke it—also just a little bit. At least I knew I could feel again. And that's when I decided that maybe juggling wasn't for me. If there was one man like Joel out there, I figured maybe there was another. One I would want to be with exclusively. I know I keep saying that it's "just dating," and that's absolutely true. It's also your life. And the life lessons we get to learn are absolutely priceless if we stay open to them.

It was definitely exciting and enlightening to know so many different kinds of men in so many different ways. But it was strange sometimes, too, recognizing that I loved something in all of them and wishing I could take pieces from each to create the man I was really looking for.

> The life lessons we get to learn are absolutely priceless if we stay open to them.

So this was how I spent my first post-divorce years: dating on my own terms, enjoying myself, and learning to let go of the cynicism I'd contracted just after my divorce. The quality of these men—all of whom I met online—was unbelievable. The interesting thing is, if I had been looking for someone to marry, I'd never have gone out with any of them, and they would never have dated me. Instead, I just stayed open, online, and out there, dating as often as I could while still holding down a job, taking care of my son, and building a new friendship with my ex. It's amazing I had any time left over for waxes, but that's another chapter.

> This was how I spent my first post-divorce years: dating on my own terms, enjoying myself, and learning to let go of the cynicism.

Dating is an adventure; an opportunity to meet a variety of people. I found that in discovering new people, I discovered new things about myself. That made all of the first dates, blind dates, and horror dates worthwhile.

Well, almost all of them.

Chapter 16

Let's Hear It from the Boys

My friends and I can spend hours talking about post-divorce dating, and we always laughingly come back to the same conclusion: Men are stupid (women say) and women are crazy (men say). By the way, my male friends generally agree with the women that they are stupid; they just say that their goal is to be stupid without getting caught.

Since most of you will be dating men, I thought I should take some notes so you can hear it straight from the guys. And not just any guys. I talked to great guys, not-so-great guys, smart guys, nice guys with a bad-boy streak, bad boys with a nice-guy streak, young guys, older guys, good-looking guys, strange guys, normal guys, and a couple of breathtaking guys—in other words, guys you are likely to go out with. No, you can't have their numbers (or their real names). And no, I did not sleep with all of them. Contrary to popular belief, you do not have to sleep with a guy to get him to talk. Especially about women. Off the record.

> **Men are stupid (women say) and women are crazy (men say).**

So, in no order of importance, here's what some real men want you to know about dating, about the guy mentality, and about what they have figured out so far about women (which takes up just one really short paragraph).

Let's start with the first date.

What Guys Look For on a First Date

Every guy told me that the way a woman looks is really important on a first date. No surprise there. What is surprising is that they don't all think the super-skinny supermodel look is hot. Well, they think it's hot, but they think a lot of things are hot. That little bulge in your stomach? They love it. That extra bit of booty? If you could walk in backward, they'd applaud it. Those laugh lines or love handles or gray hairs you can't stand? They don't even notice them unless you point them out. (So don't.) Whatever you've got, if you wear it proud they're buying it.

Evan told me he enjoys being with a woman who feels beautiful—whether he thinks she is or not—because it shows in the way she talks, walks, dances, kisses. Bill says he'll take a semi-attractive woman with brains and wit over a gorgeous airhead any day. And every single guy said the first thing they notice in a woman is her eyes, then her smile, then her breasts. Okay, sometimes they notice the breasts first. They're guys, remember?

> Whatever you've got, if you wear it proud they're buying it.

What *don't* guys like on a date? When you order a salad. Get a burger. Apparently it's very sexy to see you eat meat.

Too much makeup was a unanimous turn-off. Makes guys wonder what you really look like in the morning. They do like it when you look happy and in good physical shape (that's how Rick put it). They also love it when you laugh at their jokes. (Good, because we like it when you're actually funny.)

Keith says he really enjoys a first date. "It's the unknown. It's got a little thrill factor to it. But I also like it when it works out—I can relax a little. I don't have to be exceptional every time." (Uh, actually, yes you do.)

Jerry says screw the typical first date. "If you want to find out what your girl is really like, take her to the shooting range. Does she own her own gun? Where does she aim? What's her stance like? A girl goes with me to the range, it shows she isn't afraid of any situation; that she can handle whatever comes her way. That. Is. Hot."

Ryan says he can tell on the first date if the woman is someone with marriage potential. "How?" I demand. He lists the ways:

- "Little things, like if there are long pauses in the conversation. Don't make me work so hard to fill those pauses.

- "There has to be banter.

- "If she laughs, that's good. But if she has a grating laugh, I'm out of there.

- "If she's mean to the waiter or to my friends, I can't put up with that. No matter how good-looking a girl is, there is always someone who's tired of putting up with her. She may be hot but you still have to *like* her.

- "Is she realistic? Has she been inoculated or does she still believe in the fairy tale?"

This is Ryan's marriage potential test? My twelve-year-old niece could pass that test. Except for maybe the last one. That last one is why Ryan prefers women with a little experience; baggage even. He says women who've been "inoculated" know that no guy is perfect, that relationships take work, and that kids, jobs, families, and exes are all part of the mix.

"I'm not looking to save someone, to carry her off into the sunset. I want it to be a great relationship, but I also know that nothing is great 24/7."

Dean says that women tend to be too giving in the beginning. "Guys like a challenge. We like a woman who has some attitude, who can hold her own, who's smart and sassy." (Yes, Dean actually said sassy.) "If a guy is intimidated by your strong personality, then you don't want to be with him anyway, do you? And don't worry, younger guys will go in; they're confident."

So what makes a date go bad? Art says when women come off needy or desperate, or if they're just looking for a sperm donor or a sugar daddy. (Note to self: Stop bringing college tuition comparison on dates.) He also says sometimes you have to listen to what they're *not* saying.

"Watch out when a girl says, 'I'm not into games,'" Art explains. "That translates into 'I play a lot of games.'"

Greg doesn't like a girl who seems materialistic—one who talks about the kind of car she drives or purse she wants or places she shops. "I know this is not the girl for me. I'm already supporting an ex who likes that stuff."

The guys also say a girl shouldn't spend a lot of time talking about her ex or kids on a first date, or quizzing the guy about his. But they don't like it either when a girl has nothing to say. "You gotta bring some conversation to the table," Evan says. "Be funny. Be charming. Be radical, whatever. But I can't be the one doing all the talking."

Justin says one of his most memorable first dates was when he got into a fight with a girl over video games. She thought men over thirty who played them were immature; he had a dozen reasons why guys bond this way.

"Guys may have friends, but it's nothing like the way girls have friends. We don't say we're best friends or that we even like them. We have friends that are guys we used to know or guys who *used* to be our friends. We count them as our friends even if we haven't seen them since grade school. So when we get together, we're either out drinking beers and looking for chicks or we're in drinking beers and playing video games."

Jerry says the difference between guys and girls is that a guy falls for a girl because of who she is—what she looks like physically first, then who she turns out to be: her personality, character,

> "Women fall for who they think a guy *might* turn out to be."

intelligence, humor. "Women fall for who they think a guy *might* turn out to be. Especially once they have sex." According to Jerry, that's when a woman starts wanting to change the guy. "This is the difference: A guys says, 'Does she fit me?' A girl says, 'Can I squeeze him in?'"

Renaud adds, "Women tend to move quickly in the beginning of a relationship; they want to get close too fast. And then they confuse sex with love. Men do *not* equate sex with love. Sex is a strong component in a relationship but it doesn't equal love."

Why it Doesn't Work Out

With these kinds of differences, it's not surprising that so many relationships don't last; what's surprising is that *any* of them do. What makes a relationship go wrong? Renaud says, "Women give way too much emotionally early on. Men take much longer to give emotionally, and women push for it. That will drive us away, because we absolutely can't give it at the same pace as women.

"But once a man is into a woman, he feels it, he shows it," Renaud continues. "He *gives* her things. That's another way we're different, especially guys my age [forty-seven]. Women give their feelings

> It's not surprising that so many relationships don't last; what's surprising is that *any* of them do.

and support. Men are more comfortable giving things—we adorn our women. They just don't get it."

(Wait. Time-out. Which women are complaining about men giving them things to show they care? Check their genderhood, will you?)

Jerry goes back to the fact that women are crazy. "I was in this one relationship where I had to keep proving my love. I really liked this girl—she was my type physically, she was smart, she was usually laid-back. But I couldn't keep up with what she wanted."

I ask for an example.

"Okay, I'd had tickets for months to a Bruce Springsteen concert in New York—my buddies and I planned to go long before I started dating this girl." (Just for the record, I hate stories that involve "my buddies.")

"There was nothing I could do about it," Jerry says. "I tried to get another ticket to the concert but it was sold out. So I said to my girlfriend, 'Hey, why don't you come anyway? We'll be together all weekend, in the hotel, hanging out with friends, except for during the concert. If you have friends in New York, you can hang out with them, go shop, whatever, and I'll meet up with you after the concert.'

"Well, it was exhausting! She was never happy; not with the hotel, not with being in New York, not with hanging out with me or my friends. She just kept talking about the amount of time I would be away at the concert and not with her! You know, I realized I'd be trying to prove myself to her forever. After that trip, I was done."

The BreakUp

Ryan tells me that guys are not very good at breaking up. (Big shock there, I know.) He says it's because guys want to let themselves off the hook and out of the relationship but they don't want to be the bad guy. It's the same hormone or chromosome or whatever that makes guys say they will call you when they have no intention of calling. They think they are being polite when really they are just being a wuss.

> Guys are not very good at breaking up. (Big shock there, I know.)

Jerry says a guy's best breakup line is usually pretty lame, something like, "I'm not looking to date at the moment." (Oh, really? Then why are we out on this date? I think the next time a guy says something like this, I'm going to say, "I'm not looking to date, either. I'm looking for a hot, no-strings-attached sexual relationship. But darn, I wanted to go on a few dates first. Oh, well. See ya.")

Ryan thinks that part of the reason men are such shits is that women allow them to be. "Men set themselves up to date on a consumptive basis—quantity, not quality—and women give it to them!

"Yep, any sex is good," Justin adds. "We have a collector mentality: The more the better. And girls let us get away with it. Then they complain about it to each other. Women are good about giving advice to other women, but they're not good at taking it themselves." (Now, that might be the most insightful thing I've heard a man say about a woman in a long time.)

Which brings us to the fallback line that women love to say about guys who break up with them: "He's afraid of commitment." Greg wants you to know that "guys are *not* afraid of commitment, they may just be afraid of committing to *you*."

> "**Women are good about giving advice to other women, but they're not good at taking it themselves.**"

He says, "From pretty early on in the relationship, a guy knows in the back of his mind whether he wants to be with you forever or if you are just someone to spend time with until the right woman comes along. No matter what he says, he knows."

So how can we determine what our guy is really thinking in the back of his mind since the lying sack is telling us he'll love us forever? According to Rick, the telltale sign is if he flirts with other girls when he's with you. Man, this seems so obvious when you see it in black-and-white, doesn't it? But how many of us have been out with a guy and he's talking up our friends or the waitress and we confront him later that night and he's like, "No way, baby—I don't even remember what she looked like. I'm only into you." And we go, "Oh, okay. My bad."

The thing is, guys don't think there's anything wrong with dating an "in-between girl" or a GFN (Good For Now). And let's face it: We've heard plenty of girls describe their boyfriends as

> Guys don't think there's anything wrong with dating an "in-between girl."

"Mr. Right Now." Rick says that guys dating a GFN are basically thinking, *Why break up with her if I don't have anyone else?*

And guys think *we're* crazy? "I'll tell you why girls are crazy," Keith says. "You'll be dating a woman you really like for three months, and everything is fine. So as a guy we think, *Keep doing what you're doing.* But the woman thinks you need to up the ante, take things further somehow. Why would we change something that's going good?"

"Women my age are bitter," says Greg, who's thirty-five. "Bitter is the new bitch. I like a challenging woman, but not a bitch."

Something good must happen to us in ten years, though, because Renaud thinks women his age are better nurturers and easier to be with. "I look for a woman who's sweet," he says. "I notice how she treats me, how she interacts with my kids. You can't fake being a nurturer."

So what quality got the most votes for what a guy looks for in a long-term relationship? Trust. The guys said they need to be able to trust a woman with their kids, their work problems, their feelings, their stuff. And they need to feel that the woman trusts them. But then, the men admitted that they tend to screw that part up.

> What quality got the most votes for what a guy looks for in a long-term relationship? Trust.

"We really do," laughs Ryan. "A guy will be dating a girl and suddenly he realizes he's attracted to her best friend. The guy thinks, *I can do this*. Logically, he really believes he can do it."

There is no woman on Earth who thinks the guy can do this. Not without being a complete asshole.

And speaking of best friends . . . Evan says a girl's friends are a huge part of dating her. "If she has really bitchy friends, it can be a deal-breaker."

We've all heard of the "cock-blocker," right? (If you haven't, it's a girlfriend who doesn't let a guy get close to you—either because she's being protective, or because she's jealous, or because she's just a bitch.)

"Most girls expect you to be an ass," says Dean, "so you're basically digging yourself out of a hole to begin with. That attitude from a girl's friends is not attractive."

Art chimes in, "Look, if a guy is really interested, nothing will stop him. But women will sometimes put up obstacles that may be more than what I can or want to do."

> **"Women will sometimes put up obstacles that may be more than what I can or want to do."**

Okay, the next thing I'm about to tell you got unanimous agreement from all of the guys I interviewed, and it alone is worth the price of admission.

What is the number one reason that a guy breaks up with a girl? He's met someone else or he thinks he *may* have met someone else.

But guys typically won't tell you that this is the reason. They will say they aren't ready for a relationship or they need some space or they are moving to the Ukraine. (Is there still a Ukraine?) But ten out of ten guys said that the reason a guy breaks up with a woman is usually another woman.

Oh, and by the way? Apparently this does not preclude the guy from still wanting to have sex with you until he's sure. And that could take a while . . .

Chapter 17

Post-Divorce Dating with Kids

(Well, not taking kids ON your dates, that's just dumb)

(While this chapter is written for the single mom who has decided to start dating after her divorce or breakup, it's also fine reading for women who date men with children or men who date women with children or women who date and want children someday or basically anyone who ever was a children. Oops. Child.)

YOU MIGHT THINK THAT ALL IT TAKES FOR SINGLE MOMS to post-divorce date safely, happily, and healthily is a little common sense. Well, if you didn't throw into the mix the unpredictability of toddlers, the raging hormones of adolescents (and sometimes their mothers), the instability of new relationships, the imperfection of human nature, and the fact that there is no bible on the topic, then yes, a little common sense would be all you need.

But it also takes some understanding, patience, flexibility, and a large sense of humor. Over the years I've spoken with several family therapists and I try to keep up with the latest research;

I thought I would offer you the top suggestions for healthy post-divorce dating with kids.

Of course, while I was doing this research I was horrified to learn how many things I've already done that I should have done differently, so now I'm wondering if the therapy trust fund I set up for my son is going to be enough or if I will have to take out a second mortgage on my home. Try not to worry if you're not doing everything the way some of the experts suggest. Every child is different; every parent is different; every divorce is way different. There is no one right way to date after divorce; I think it's really all about treating yourself and your children with respect. If we can remember to do that, I think we'll all be okay. Even our kids.

> There is no one right way to date after divorce; I think it's really all about treating yourself and your children with respect.

One thing that keeps me balanced is remembering that I'm a mother first. (This is why my son thinks he is the center of the universe—because for a little while longer, he is.) As I started dating, I tried to consider my son's needs and feelings first, and mine second. For me, this was a good guideline.

A lot of women simply keep their dating life private, separate from their family life. Most experts agree that children do not need to be involved at all. That's because it can be really confusing—especially for young children—to introduce them to a revolving door of dates. And don't let your sulky indifferent older child fool you; teenagers can also have mixed emotions or feel misunderstood when their mothers begin to date.

Here are some tips from family therapists, marriage counselors, and experienced divorced daters. And of course, my two cents:

- **Your children should not meet your dates.** Instead, drive your own car and meet your date out somewhere. Another option is to date only when you don't have your kids for the night or the weekend or the summer or whatever. (Even then, don't have a date pick you up at your home until you know him well enough for him to know where you live. This could be several months or more.) If you get a babysitter, don't discuss with your children that you are going on a date. Don't discuss it with the babysitter, either.

- **Be conscious of how your children feel when you go out.** Do they seem clingy? Angry? Thrilled? (Thrilled would be the sixteen-year-olds. Hide the car keys.) Children and especially teenagers may not tell us that they want to be with us, but their true feelings may show up in other ways. If you do date when your kids are with you, be sensitive to how much you date on "their time."

> Children and especially teenagers may not tell us that they want to be with us, but their true feelings may show up in other ways.

- **Keep private things private.** Most therapists and divorced parents agree that sleepovers should be kept to nights that the kids are not at home, and only when you are in a serious relationship. Be discreet. You don't know how your neighbors are going to react to seeing a car in your driveway . . . or how your neighbors' kids will react and what they may say to your children.

- **Consider how to introduce your kids to someone who's become important to you.** (Isn't there a better word than *boyfriend*? Seriously, I feel like an idiot using this word at this stage of my life.) Therapists agree on a few best practices: When you do introduce your boyfriend to your children, meet on neutral ground—not at your house, not at his house, not at your ex's house when you pick up your kids. Meet at a park, a restaurant, a sporting event—something casual. Introduce your new friend as just that—a friend— then continue to talk to your children about him in the weeks ahead. Slowly, let your children know that he is more than a friend, but keep the details and any talk about the future to yourself. Assure your kids that no matter how you and your boyfriend feel about each other, your children come first.

- **By the way, you don't ever have to introduce a guy to your kids.** If the man you are dating is pushing to meet your kids, that's a red flag. These are your kids, your protection, your decision. Ask yourself why your boyfriend is forcing this. Men (and women) have been known to use kids to manipulate a relationship and get closer. Don't do it.

- **Explaining a breakup.** So let's say you've taken your time, you have a serious boyfriend, you've kept the sleepovers private, you've introduced him to your kids, you've all spent time together, and then *wham!* You break up. Apparently this can be as traumatic (or more) for your kids as it is for you, no matter what age they are. Kids get attached; they get comfortable with a new setup because it helps them feel secure. Now their world is changing again. Not to mention your children will likely miss the boyfriend—he may have become someone important in their lives, too. Even when you do everything right, this is still a real possibility. Things happen. Uh, you're divorced, remember? Be sensitive to your children's feelings. Talk to them about the breakup honestly and age-appropriately, and try not to let them see you break down. You're the grown-up.

- **Keep the conversation open.** Your children are going to turn to you for honest answers. How do you know how much to say? If you don't tell your kids that you're dating at all, then they may feel betrayed when you tell them you're seeing someone seriously. If you introduce

> A breakup can be almost as traumatic for your kids as it is for you.

them to every guy you date, they may feel scared and confused. The most important thing is to remind your kids that you are there for them first and foremost, and that their world is safe. When the time is right, let them know that you may start dating again, that you will be making new friends. But reassure your children that no relationship is more important than the one you have with them—and let your actions prove it.

> **Remind your kids that you are there for them first and foremost, and that their world is safe.**

- **Don't feel guilty about dating. Don't feel guilty about not dating.** And don't feel guilty if you have to cancel a date because something came up with your child. Most adults understand that plans get broken at the last minute when a child gets sick or your ex has to go out of town. If your date isn't cool with this, he's probably not the right guy.

- **Be supportive of your ex dating.** Let your kids know that you are okay with it, that you want their dad to be happy. If *you're* not dating yet, now might be a good time to tell your children that you may date when you're ready. Be upbeat and positive; you don't want your child to feel sorry for you or for your ex; you do not want your children to feel as if they have to take care of you, either. That can really mess up a kid. Trust me.

- **Yes, you can have a personal life.** You may even go through a wild phase after your divorce. Just be safe and do *not* subject your children to it. Don't constantly talk to or text your boyfriend in front of your kids. Don't invite your boyfriend to every meal, soccer game, birthday party, and so on. Your children will become adults someday (with any luck) and they will start dating someone and this will all come back to haunt you.

- **Be discreet.** A lot of children feel uncomfortable seeing their mom kiss another man, even if it's just on the cheek. Watch for how your children react, and respect their feelings. A kiss on the cheek or a hug is usually okay, especially after you have been serious with a man for a long time and your kids are comfortable with him. But even those mild displays of affection can create feelings of fear, confusion, or just the "ick" factor.

- **Never criticize your ex's girlfriend in front of your children.** Never criticize your own boyfriend in front of your children. Never criticize your ex's girlfriend's ex-boyfriends in front of your children. See? Adult relationships are complex—even we adults mess them up. Your kids don't need to know why someone broke up with you, or if he was cheating on you, or if he was spending too much time online, or whatever. If you and your boyfriend break up, gently let your children know that you won't be seeing each other anymore. This would be a good time to tell your children (again) that your relationship with them will never go away.

- **Your new significant other (SO) is not your child's father and he shouldn't act like one**—whether he is at your home or you are all out together. Talk with your boyfriend about how you'd like him to behave around your children; give him suggestions about the input he should or shouldn't have. It's not easy, and it will take some time. Your boyfriend is part guest, part friend, but he *is* an adult. If he sees your child doing something unsafe, expect him to intervene. But if you and your child are having an argument, you may not want your boyfriend to step in. That can make your child feel as if the two of you are ganging up on him, or that you are siding with your boyfriend and disrespecting your child's feelings. Don't cop out on your role as a parent.

> This would be a good time to tell your children (again) that your relationship with them will never go away.

- **Talk to your kids. Love your kids. Respect your kids. Spend time with your kids.** If you want to wait until your children are older before you date, then wait. If you date a little or a lot, if you stop dating and start and stop again, don't worry. There will be plenty of opportunities to date. Pretty soon your kids will be grown and they won't be living at home anymore (God willing). And no, you won't be too old to date, no matter what your kids say.

- **If you've already started dating, and you're doing things differently than the suggestions here, don't stress** (like I did). Especially if it's all going well. You know by now that every situation is different; every child is unique. If you think some of these suggestions are better than what you're doing now, use them. I think the finest thing you can do is to simply keep your children's best interests at heart while you are learning to open yours up again.

- **Don't do anything too stupid.**

Getting Un-Pissed-Off

One of the best ways *not* to mess up our kids has nothing to do with dating. It has everything to do with being a mature ex-wife. To me that means being supportive of your kids' dad. Being flexible when his plans change. Being a responsible mother. Being a consistent co-parent. Not using your kids as ammunition or spies. And for a lot of us, that means letting go of the anger.

What good is the anger anyway? It does not burn enough calories to make you thinner. It will not make you more attractive. It will waste your precious time and energy—energy you could be using to do something good for yourself.

Yes, I hear you. Your ex was a jerk. A lying jerk. A lying, cheating, lazy jerk. Or he was the greatest guy and the love of your life and he threw it all away in some stupid midlife crisis. It hurts, I know. I do not want to minimize that. But you are continuing to hurt yourself and your relationship with your children if you stay so pissed off.

Hate is Not the Opposite of Love

My dad is a court mediator. That means he helps people figure out a way to solve their problems without using expensive lawyers or court time. One day he's telling me about a divorce case he has. The divorce has been going on, unresolved, for five years, and the couple and their lawyers have agreed to see a mediator.

Now, my dad has been married to my mom for fifty-one years, and he has four kids and eight grandkids. He knows a little something about what it takes to stay married. But he's also real old-school and has kind of a *just get over it* mentality. So he's listening to both sides of the story—what the wife wants, what the husband wants, what the wife thinks, what the husband thinks of what the wife thinks—and the husband and wife start going at it, arguing loudly and gesturing and knocking things over. My dad finally interrupts them and says in a low voice, "So how long have the two of you been in love?"

The couple is speechless—but only for a second. They start yelling at my dad, one louder than the other: "In love? Are you kidding? I hate him! I can't stand her! She's the devil!" Stuff like that.

My dad says, "Then why in the world have you been meeting once a month for five years and bringing up all these old stories over and over again? If you really hate each other that much, why doesn't one of you just sign the papers and move on? You don't have children, you're not living together, you'll never have to see each other again."

It's quiet in the courthouse while this sinks in. My dad goes on, "You know, hate is not the opposite of love. Apathy is. Hate is pretty passionate. I don't see how you can move on if you're holding on to that much passion."

The lawyers are about to slug my father, but the husband speaks up. "Wow." That's all he says. Then he gets up and leaves.

I don't know what ever happened to that couple. Did they get back together? Did one of them finally sign the papers? Did they continue going back to court month after month? I don't know. But I think that my dad was dead-on about hate. He told me later that he thinks anger causes a kind of illness in a person, and he always counsels people to try to let it go.

> "I don't see how you can move on if you're holding on to that much passion."

So do yourself a favor (and make my dad happy): Let go of the anger. It really is not going to do you any good, and in fact, it could cause you harm. It can raise your stress level, your blood pressure, and it causes those really ugly little creases by your mouth. If you don't want your ex consuming your life anymore, don't let him.

Forgive him. (And maybe that means forgiving yourself, too.) I'm not saying you will forget whatever it is he's done; in fact, remember to put it in your Manfile. But don't hold on to that burning anger. It's not good for your children, either. The reality is that sometimes people screw up and things don't work out. But it's better to show your kids (and yourself) that the way you handle the bad stuff life hands you is really the definition of who you are.

An Opportunity to See What You're Made Of

I felt that I had every right to be pissed and resentful and self-righteous when I divorced my ex. And I was, for a little while. But I also saw my divorce as an opportunity to flex my best character. Sure I got mad, especially in the beginning. But then I would dig deep and find some forgiveness. Some compassion. Some *grace*. For both of us. Talk about exhausting! Yet the more I did it, the more I showed myself what I was really made of. I used those qualities that God gave me on reserve for just such an occasion. So even when I did things wrong, I really tried to love myself for stretching and being the best I could—better than I knew I could be.

My ex did a lot of growing and stretching, too. Shit, he went into rehab! And I am grateful. But letting go of the anger is what helped me create a strong and true friendship with my ex. Unless he starts dating some bimbo, and then all bets are off.

Without the anger, you can move on. After all, the best revenge is living a life that makes you happy.

Chapter 18

Dating Your Exes, Your Friends' Exes, and the Not-Yet Exes

NO ONE COULD CALL ATLANTA A SMALL TOWN, BUT WE HAVE a bunch of suburbs and neighborhoods that are very . . . *neighborly.* The one I live in is sort of *Desperate Housewives* meets *Touched by an Angel.* It's big enough that we don't all know everything about one another, but small enough that when we run into a woman at the grocery store who is wearing something other than a tennis outfit and actually has makeup on, we assume she's single like us (why else would she look nice just to go to the grocery store?) and that we know her. Or we know her ex. Or her not-quite-yet ex.

It happened to me just the other night. I was with my date at a Latin restaurant we go to often enough to know the bartender's name. As I wiggle my way in between two barstools, I hear someone squeal my name. I look to my left and see Laura, a woman I met last month when we were out with mutual friends. As I go to give her a hug, I look down to see her holding hands with the man sitting next to her. This is Brandon, a guy I met several months ago when I was out with a different group of friends. So I had been out with each of them at different times, different places, with different groups of friends—*and not once had either of them mentioned that they were married.* In fact, it becomes clear as we say our hellos that neither of them knows that the other one has ever met me.

As I move to give Laura a hug, Brandon thinks I'm saying hello to him and he gives me a hug. So we're in this kind of three-way hug and the two of them pull away and say at the same time, "You know Ginger?"

Which I take as my cue to introduce them to my date. Fortunately, neither one of them appears to know him. That would really be cluttered.

So Brandon asks me, "How do you know Laura?" just as Laura asks me, "How do you know Brandon?"

What are Your Relationship Rules?

I usually like to give these questions a really big pause, in case the person I am being asked about wants to jump in and answer. I have no idea what their situation is and really, neither of them had done anything bad in my book, but how do I know that going out to bars is okay in *their* book of relationship rules? Sure, Brandon was doing some heavy flirting with my table of girlfriends the night we met, while Laura wasn't exactly deflecting come-ons from guys the night I was out with her. But they both went home alone, to the best of my knowledge.

My big pause doesn't work in this situation, because they both asked a question at the same time and now they are looking at me expectantly.

"Well, let's see," I say, looking at no one in particular. "I know we met out with some friends of friends, right? Weren't you both there?" I ask, channeling my sometimes Alzheimer's.

Brandon steps up and says, "Yeah, we met at Brio one night when the guys and I were having drinks."

This is not exactly accurate but I don't argue.

Laura recalls that we met at a Girls' Night Out but she says she can't remember where. I'm thinking she definitely remembers where, but the where might not thrill Brandon, since it involved the kind of girl-stuff usually reserved for bachelorette parties, and there were no bachelorettes with us. (And really, why should brides-to-be have all the fun? I can go to the same places and have big fun without wearing a bridal veil and carrying around a margarita glass shaped like a penis.)

I could tell the two of them were wondering what the other one had said and done and revealed to me on those nights, because they were eyeing each other and they had dropped the hand-holding thing.

"Well, it's really nice running into both of you," I say. "We're going to dance."

And with that, my date and I take off. Later he asked me where I had really met them.

Enter the Truth

"Well, I met Laura when a group of *my* friends and a group of *her* friends were out one night and we all decided to go to Max's [a place where one side has female strippers and the other side has male strippers].

"I met Brandon when some of my girlfriends and I were out dancing late one night at Lococos. I do think Brandon and his buddies had been to Brio earlier, but that had been several drinks ago."

There's more, so I continue. "Laura's really outgoing and guys were offering her dollar bills to dance," I explain.

"Did she?" my date asks.

"Uh, yes, but she didn't take anything off, if that's what you're wondering."

My date looks disappointed.

"Brandon is pretty charming and he was flirting with all of us, but I saw him leave with his friends. I think it was just a couple of marrieds stepping out a little to the left of innocent, but I definitely didn't want to be caught in the middle of he said/she said," I say.

What *is* the proper protocol for running into married people whom you met when they weren't acting married?

The Not-quite-yet Ex

The next week, my friend Jennie went out with her own group of single girlfriends, which is different from going out with your married girlfriends or even a group of half-and-half. Sometimes your single friends will bring other single friends so it's not like you always know everyone there (which is exactly how I had met Laura).

Anyway, Jennie tells me that she's at the restaurant meeting all the other girlfriends of girlfriends, and she shakes hands with a woman who looks vaguely familiar but she can't place her. They start chatting and realize that their kids go to the same school. When Jennie gets up to use the ladies' room, her close friend Maria follows her in.

"Don't you know who that *is?*" Maria practically bursts.

"I just met her," Jennie says. "Sally something, right?"

"Uh, yeah, Sally something," Maria hisses. "Don't you know she went out with Rick a couple of times last month?"

Rick is Jennie's ex-husband.

"She did?" Jennie asks, but it's rhetorical. She mulls this over, shrugs, and heads back out.

Girls Will Be Girls

As soon as she gets back to the girls' table, Jennie looks for Sally and waves her over. She bends her head toward her ear and, in a conspiratorial voice, says, "I just remembered who you are."

Sally looks at her with wide eyes; she obviously knows who Jennie is, too. She doesn't know if Jen is going to scream or cry or pity her. As it turns out, Jennie feels . . . nothing.

"I just didn't want it to be awkward," Jennie tells the woman. "I'm totally okay with whoever Rick wants to date—he and I are friends; I wish him the best. Anyway," Jennie adds, "your ex asked me out last year—that makes us kind of even, right?"

Sally gives her a blank stare. Her bottom lip is quivering, and Jennie is trying to figure out what she said that's made her go white as a sheet.

"You okay?" Jennie asks.

Sally takes one step backward, as if Jen has suddenly turned into a bloodsucking zombie.

"My ex asked you out last year?!" Sally practically shrieks. "We just got divorced six months ago!"

WTF? Jennie thinks. This is not proper post-divorce dating. It's not even post-divorce anything. It's pre-divorce bad behavior: exes asking out women before they are even exes.

It happens all the time, but most of the time neither the askee nor the almost divorced wife ever finds out. That would only happen in a small town, right? But Jennie hadn't had any idea; she figured here's this woman who dated her ex, she's divorced. She hadn't considered for how long.

"Oh, well, I'm sorry then," Jennie says. "If it makes you feel any better, I didn't go out with him."

Sally turns on her heel and walks out.

Damn, Jennie says to herself. *I guess that didn't make her feel any better.*

Dating Your Friend's Exes . . . Once They *Are* Exes

Every once in a while, a friend or an acquaintance or a colleague will say to me, "You ought to date my ex-husband—he's a great guy." Which begs the question, *Then why did you divorce him?* I don't ask, because I've tried to set friends up with my ex a few times, too. It's complicated why we can love an ex from afar, and why we would offer him up to a girlfriend who might truly fit him better.

But really, the question isn't, *Should I date your ex?* The question is, *What will happen to our friendship if I date your ex?* And the answer almost always is, *It will go to hell.* That's because most people, no matter how open-minded we are, are pretty possessive, and the thinking is: *Just because I don't want him doesn't mean I want you to have him.* This is typically true even if your friend says it's okay; it doesn't bother her, she couldn't care less. Even if she is the one who suggested it! It almost always doesn't turn out well. And by the way, once a friend's ex wants *you*, suddenly he's very attractive to that friend again. Now, there's some psychological shit.

How many of us have secretly (or not-so-secretly) coveted a friend's boyfriend or husband once they've broken up? It makes sense: She's your friend because you like each other and have a lot in common; if she liked him, it stands to reason that you would probably like him, too. Plus, you may already be friends with her ex, and that makes the transition to new boyfriend seem easier.

> The thinking is: *Just because I don't want him doesn't mean I want you to have him.*

It's not. It may make sense in a human-nature kind of way. . . but this is the stuff reality shows can't wait to catch on tape.

Now, I'm not saying that dating a friend's ex never works out; I do have a friend or two who have dated friends' exes with no nuclear fallout. But typically these were very, very amicable exes; exes where the split was mutual and no one felt dumped; exes that had already clearly moved on. That is a best-case scenario.

The one piece of advice I have about dating a friend's ex is to weigh the risks against the benefits: Is this guy really worth losing your friend over? Because that is a real possibility; maybe even a probability. Each case is different: How close are you with the friend? How serious are you about the ex and his qualities? How will you feel if you're all at a party together one night? How will you feel if it doesn't work out and you've now lost a boyfriend and a friend?

> Weigh the risks against the benefits: Is this guy really worth losing your friend over?

For the most part, I believe that there are enough guys out there that we don't have to date each other's exes. Although some days, it does seem pretty slim.

Those are the days that I say forget about my girlfriends' exes; maybe I'll just date my girlfriends.

Dating Your Own Ex

They are called redaters and recouplers: people who are married or together for months or years or more, break up, and get back together again. Sometimes exes get back together for a night, sometimes for another long-term relationship, and sometimes for good. Can you, should you, dare you date your own ex? Plenty of people do. Sometimes they're just looking for a casual hookup once in a while. But if you want more than sex with your ex, you should know that the most common mistake couples make when redating is not giving the breakup enough time.

You need time to assess what went wrong. You need time to work on your own issues. You need time to heal if it was a bad breakup. And you need time to answer some serious questions: Has your ex really changed? Are your expectations different this time around? Have you put the past behind you or do you keep dredging it up? Can you both talk about this stuff freely and openly, without yelling or storming out of the house? Does he still drive you crazy (in a good way) or does he just make you insane? It takes time just to ask these questions, much less answer them.

There are a few reasons *not* to date an ex: Because it's easier than trying to find someone new. Because your next-door neighbor's sister is about to date him. Because you're lonely. Or horny. Or broke. These are not the building blocks of a lasting relationship.

You already know that no relationship is perfect; dating your ex is like proving that theory. My best advice is that if both of you think you were truly meant for each other and you want to try again, go for it. Just wait a few months.

And don't leave any naked pictures of you behind. You don't want them showing up on mynakedexGF.com. Again.

Chapter 19

Finding Your Sensual Goddess

A FRIEND OF MINE INTRODUCED ME TO A "SENSUAL massage therapist" shortly after my marriage ended. She'd read about it in a women's magazine (ironically called *O*). Or maybe she saw it on a porn site—she couldn't remember. Anyway, she told me it would help me get my "feminine mystique" back. I don't know why she thought I needed this kind of help. Maybe I was one of those women whom other women talk about behind their backs and say things like, "Wow, she is in such a bad mood. She needs to get laid." I myself haven't said that about anyone for at least twenty years. There are so many other things a moody woman might need. She might need a Prozac. She might need a manicure. She might need a housekeeper. But apparently, I needed help managing my mojo.

Because I had not been remotely sensual for longer than most women go without getting a physical—even longer than those of you who put off going to the doctor for a really, really long time—this seemed like something I might actually need.

But how was a sensual massage therapist going to help me? Would it be like a regular massage or more like what I fantasize about when I'm getting a regular massage? Would I have to be naked or was it something he could coach me through with my clothes on? Turns out, it was both. And it turns out that the he was a she.

Reducing Our Bitch Factor

Her name was Yani, and she put me at ease immediately. Yani was actually a Sensuality Goddess—she had a certificate in it and everything. She believed in the power and strength of women and that if our sensuality was blocked it could wreak havoc on our mind, health, and soul. It could also make us bitchy.

Okay. I got that. I was humming right along with the Goddess when Graham walked into the room. Graham is Yani's partner in her sensual massage therapy business. (Even Goddesses gotta earn a living. This was a business with a capital *B*, although it was colored in pale purple with glitter and butterflies.) Yani introduced me to Graham and said she thought it would be good for both of them to work with me today. She and Graham had worked together for years to help women recapture their sensuality, achieve their sexual freedom, and, for some women, attain the elusive orgasm.

Well, I didn't have many inhibitions—I was just born free, I guess. But I had been in forced celibacy for a very long time. Did I really need this to move forward? Even with my Freebird attitude, I was hesitant to receive the four-hand massage that Graham and Yani were talking about during our thirty-minute consultation—the part of the session that happens while your clothes are still on.

We didn't just talk about the sensual massage; we talked about my family, my work, my dreams; where I was in my post-divorce journey; and, of course, if I wanted to set my inner goddess free. Graham and Yani were both life coaches as well as massage therapists, and they had very interesting and outside-the-box perspectives on sex and sensuality. I was starting to be swayed. Theoretically, of course.

Then Yani stood and told me to follow her. We went into a lovely spa-like room containing a massage table, a fireplace, flowers and a large shower stall. She asked me to lie facedown on the table. So far, so good—just like a secular massage.

> By the time the session was over, I indeed felt rejuvenated, lighter, and almost as if I'd actually had sex.

Before I knew it, Yani was speaking softly, chanting mantras about women and wives and Mother Earth and . . . I don't know, Father Time? I could hear her telling Graham what to do—pressure points here and Swedish massage there. It was very relaxing and kind of surreal.

By far the hardest part of the massage was when Yani asked me to hold her hand and look into her eyes. Have you ever noticed how intimate it is to look into someone's eyes and not say anything, not pull back your hand, not make some attempt at humor, but just quietly stare at her? Or him? It was uncomfortable for me. Lesson one.

Yani continued to rub oils onto my skin, to work my muscles and massage my head. She offered prayers and thanks and I felt as if I were having an out-of-body experience. It was heavenly.

By the time the session was over, I indeed felt rejuvenated, lighter, and almost as if I'd actually had sex. If I could remember what that was like.

The only thing was, I had tears streaming down my face. That usually doesn't happen to me—post-massage or post-coital or post-Prada, for that matter. Yani and Graham smiled like angels and left the room. I got up and showered and dressed and we all returned to the garden to talk. They were still smiling at me like benevolent parents at a kindergarten recital.

"How do you feel?" Yani asked. I checked in with myself: Relaxed. Happy. Hopeful.

"Sensual?" she asked.

"Hmm," I said, pondering, "I feel . . . *taller*," and I laughed. So much for sharing intimate moments.

I thought about why I had been crying and realized that just the simple touch of another human being after not being touched for so long had made me feel vulnerable and . . . grateful. I was thankful that people like Yani and Graham existed and did this work. I know it sounds flaky and outside the norm. But if any of you have gone without for a long time, I think you are probably nodding your heads and doing a search on the Internet for a sensual massage therapist in your city.

If you do find one, please be careful. There should be no sex, no pushiness, and you should feel very safe and comfortable. If you do sign up, maybe you can check out

> The simple touch of another human being after not being touched for so long had made me feel vulnerable and . . . grateful.

their references (anonymously, of course) or, hey, there's always the Better Business Bureau.

I don't know if it was coincidence or if my inner goddess was still afterglowing, but inordinate numbers of men started asking me out on dates—even online, where they couldn't possibly see my glow. Within weeks I went on my second (and much better) first date, and a few months later I began my first semi-serious relationship after my divorce.

Girls' Night In, Swingers, and Street Clothes

When I tried to contact Yani several months later to inquire about a workshop she offered, she had moved. So I called Graham, and we struck up a conversation. He invited me to have a free life-coaching session, and I did. What I really needed to know, I told him, was all about dating in the twenty-first century. Graham essentially gave me a crash course, and his was a very interesting perspective.

He introduced me to several other recently divorced women, some who were so uninhibited they did not understand the need for a glass of wine, you know what I mean? One day, Graham gave me an invitation to a party his friends were throwing—he wouldn't be there, it was all girls. Single girls. I should go to learn more about dating, he said. To get some answers. And maybe take a few pictures, he suggested with a laugh. He made it clear that *Girls Gone Wild* was PG compared with this group.

So I drive up to the address and it's a mansion—not one of

those mini-mansions, a mansion mansion. I park behind a BMW and a Mercedes, check my lipstick in the rearview mirror, and get out of my minivan. I'm so nervous I almost lock my keys in the car. I take a deep breath and walk up the stairs to the heavy mahogany doors. I start to knock, change my mind, turn and walk back down the stairs.

"Don't be such a wimp," I whisper to myself, and I walk up the stairs again. I start to knock. Turn around again. Walk back to the car. I do this about three more times until I realize my heels are making little round divots in the front lawn and now someone is standing at the front door, trying not to laugh.

She's tall, dirty blond, slim. She's beautiful even with this major gap between her front teeth, and that's what makes her approachable.

"Are you ever going to come?" she says smiling, and I think this is the start of a night of double entendres.

I have no choice now but to continue up the steps, smiling and coasting as if I was coming all along, and shake her hand, which she gently pushes away to give me a warm hug.

"You must be Ginger, Graham's friend," she says with the most adorable Australian accent. "Come on in, we've been waiting for you."

Again, I hear the smirk. Playful, but a smirk nonetheless.

I follow her past an obscenely large foyer with a grand piano, and down the marble steps to the "party room"—a basement with four large rooms, a kitchen, a bar, and a door leading out to a swimming pool. Later I will learn that there is also a "harem" room.

True to Graham's word there are only women here. But they don't look anything like my neighborhood Garden Club. There are women with tattoos, thigh-highs, biker gear, and pierced tongues. There are women in short skirts, lingerie, and one in a metallic bikini. They are playing a game where everyone had written down a question on a slip of paper and put it in a jar; whoever pulled out a question had to answer it. As I walk in, the game is suspended midpull, so everyone can come over and hug me and kiss my cheek and get me a tequila shooter. As the newcomer, I'm asked to write down a question right then and there, just as a woman named Mollie announces that she has gotten a new piercing in a very private place. There is a group "oooooo" as she steps out of her jeans to show us what looks to me like the most painful thing I can ever imagine, and I have had natural childbirth. I try not to wince.

That's when someone pulls my question out of the hat. It says simply, "What is the current style of bikini waxing?"

I have never seen so many pants go down at once in my whole life, and I used to potty-train preschoolers. Every girl there wants to show me the very latest in trendy trimming. Note to self: This is *not* your mother's bikini wax.

First up, Ellie insists that bare is the new garter belt. She's in the middle of thirty laser treatments to have all of her pubic hair removed.

"Does it hurt?" I ask, definitely wincing.

"Like a motherfucker," she says proudly.

Lucinda agrees with the bare-is-best look, but she prefers

waxing. (I hear later that she's having a fling with her aesthetician.) A few other girls say that a "landing strip" is the preferred look (preferred by men or women? I'm not sure). A landing strip is when you remove all of your pubic hair save for a strip about two inches long and half an inch wide in the very center. Except nobody at the party says pubic hair, okay?

Well, I got my answer! Completely bare or mostly bare were the only acceptable looks, unless there were additions such as tattoos or piercings. I can tell you that no one had the au naturel look that every *Playboy* centerfold from the 1950s to the 1980s sported. That's what I get for divorcing at the turn of the century.

As bizarre as this girl-party was, I really was glad for the knowledge. Who else could I have asked about trimming and tweezing and Trojans? *Now*, I thought, *if I ever do get naked again, at least I won't look like a born-again virgin.*

I reported back to Graham who, of course, said I could have just asked him. What, and missed out on the debate of hot wax versus laser? Silicone versus saline? Men versus women?

And that's when Graham said he was taking me on a field trip. Out of my comfort zone. To a swingers' club.

Now, being a writer, I have a certain overwhelming curiosity about . . . well, just about everything. I was the first company editor to ride in IBM's electronic warehouse machine, hovering six stories high for eight hours. I once drove four hours just to go dancing on top of a glass-enclosed shark pool and lived to write about it. I did my first rock climb in thirty-degree weather on my fortieth birthday and the next year tried to learn to snowboard

> Being a writer, I have a certain overwhelming curiosity about . . . well, just about everything.

in Colorado. I've written about Jews for Jesus, *Vagina Monologues,* and the transsexual talent show at Crazy Pete's. But a swingers' club? I was game for the exploration, I was just a little apprehensive about what we'd be exploring.

As soon as we walk in, we are astonished: The fee is outrageous. You have to pay for a three-month membership even if you swear you're never coming back; it's steep, purportedly, to keep the riffraff out. If all that separates the sleazy from the acceptable is a cover charge, we'd have a much different electoral process.

So we pay and we walk inside and immediately I burst out laughing. Straight ahead of me is the largest, shiniest, fullest buffet bar I have ever seen. It is a smorgasbord, really, of roasts and potatoes, veggies and casseroles, turkey breasts and gravy and fruit salad and cheesecake. Do you really want to eat from a buffet in a sex club? If I'm going to be half naked in front of people, I'm not eating for days.

Graham grabs my arm and hisses for me to stop laughing, which I do, as soon as I look on the dance floor. There are two women dancing—how can I say this?—upside down. When I look more closely, I see that they are hanging from a bar attached to the ceiling of the dance floor, and since they are upside down we can see that their mothers would be proud: They remembered the advice about clean underwear, and so they chose not to wear any at all. They are kissing several other men and women who are standing right-side up on the dance floor. This looks like an X-rated version of the upside-down kiss in the Spider-Man movie.

I turn to Graham and say I need a drink, so we go to the bar. This is when Graham remembers that this is a Bring Your Own Bottle club. He doesn't drink so he didn't think to tell me. Now we are the only sober people in a room full of people high on liquor, Ecstasy, lust, transmission fluid, who knows what else.

As I look up, I notice several large-screen TVs displaying porn movies that are so X-rated, I can't believe they don't burn up the DVD players. And here's the kicker: No one is watching them! It's like being at the big game and having other games playing on television—why watch TV when it's live in front of you? At this point I am backing up to see if I can sneak out the door, but Graham tells me to relax.

"At least everyone has their clothes on here," he says.

Here? What do you mean here? Is there a somewhere else? I don't know if it's the sight of the food or the video or the sobriety, but I'm getting a little queasy.

That's when Graham tells me that the thing I really have to see is the back room. That's the real draw, he says. I can blame my journalistic instincts all I want, but at this point I'm dying of curiosity. We head that way, but before we can enter, we see a sign that says NO STREET CLOTHES ALLOWED. I turn to Graham to ask what we're supposed to do, when a gentleman from the club says, "Sorry, guys, everyone has to store their clothes in the locker room. You'll get a white towel to wear in the back room."

"There is *no way*," I whisper to Graham. "I did not put on a black minidress and high-heeled boots to walk around in a white towel. White is not even a good color for me."

The attendant shoots me a look, so I smile at him, walk into the locker room, and take the white towel. I wrap it around my shoulders like a pashmina shawl. Graham changes into the towel. I am fully clothed, but I am also wearing my white towel. We walk out and I hold my breath. No one stops us. It seems as if women can get away with breaking the rules around here, and anyway, these are not my street clothes; these are the clothes I would wear for Halloween if I was going as a hooker. Which is frowned upon in my neighborhood.

We walk into the back room and all I see are bodies—some toweled, some gartered, some hairy, some slim, some covered, some that maybe should be covered. But the main thing I notice is that there is smoke everywhere. Apparently shoes aren't allowed back here but cigarettes are.

In fact, we can actually see a woman smoking a cigarette while she is engaged in sex. Well, I guess she's not really all that engaged, huh? She is dragging on her Marlboro while her partner is, well, you know. I am not kidding. This is *during*, not after. I'm sorry, but I believe that sex deserves more respect than that.

I turn to Graham and tell him I need to go. This scene is not for me. He laughs and asks me to chill. I think this is as chilled as I will get in this place. But then I glance over at a room that's filled with mattresses—a group room, I guess. There is a very large woman with a very large man. They are totally, enthusiastically into each other. They look extremely happy. And I think to myself, good for them. If this is what they enjoy, then they should have all the sex they want. Just not in front of me.

My next thought is that any adult who wants to have consensual sex should be able to—homely, beautiful, shy, outgoing, young, old, blond, bald, fit, not-so-fit . . . who am I to have any opinion on it at all, really? And that's when I realize: This is the sensual Goddess in me talking. I turn to Graham and tell him. He smiles and says, "My work here is done. Let's go get a burger."

I hope I didn't embarrass you with that last story (Mom and Dad). But if you read all the way through it and you are considering checking out a swingers' club, know before you go:

> "My work here is done. Let's go get a burger."

- Go with someone you know well and absolutely trust. Go home with the person you came with.

- Go as an observer your first time. You don't have to be as neurotic as I was, but it's a good idea to get the feel of the place and think about what makes you comfortable and uncomfortable before you participate.

- If you go with a boyfriend or a date, make an agreement about any and all rules ahead of time. For example, an old friend of mine goes regularly with his wife. She is allowed to kiss girls; he is only allowed to kiss her.

- I would suggest not drinking. This is not a place where you want to lose your senses.

- I definitely wouldn't eat, but plenty of people do. That's just me.

- Go only on couples' nights. Single girls do not want to go on nights when the club allows in single men, even though it is a hefty entrance fee for these guys. You will be mauled, pawed, eyed greedily. Don't do it, unless that's what you're into.

- Leave early, before everyone else has had too much . . . of everything.

- Don't do anything stupid. Really. A lot of stuff looks stupid here.

Chapter 20

On Being a Cougar

I DID NOT INTENTIONALLY START OUT TO BECOME A COUGAR. In fact, I didn't even know what a cougar was. Well, of course I knew what one was in the animal kingdom; I just didn't know what it was in the dating kingdom. In case you don't know either, *cougar* is the moniker for a woman who dates a younger man, or several younger men. I don't think it's meant to be particularly flattering, but my best friend Hope, who's five years younger than I am, insists that it's a wonderful tag. (I don't know what they call a woman whose best friend is younger than she is.)

"A cougar is sleek, confident, powerful," Hope explained to me excitedly. "She can toy with her prey if she wants to. She knows if this one gets away there will be plenty of others to come along."

Well, that's not exactly how I feel. And I'm not sure everyone else share's Hope's enthusiasm. Although I've never heard anyone make a snide remark when I'm out with my boyfriend— who is more than ten years younger than I am. (But maybe I've already lost some of my hearing.) My friends and family do tease me sometimes. And some of my friends want to know if he has a younger brother.

Curiously, I haven't heard what they call a guy who dates younger women, except maybe *lucky*. The double standard itself makes the name *cougar* offensive, I think.

Apart from a couple of guys who were my age or maybe a year older, I have always dated younger men. In fact, I married one: My ex is almost five years younger than I am.

After my divorce I dated men from several eras, but I wasn't surprised to learn that I still tended to gravitate toward younger men, particularly since I wasn't looking for anything serious. At one point I was casually dating one man who was my age, one who was nine years younger, and one who was just over thirty.

And then about a year ago, I was minding my own business (mostly) when one of the young men I was dating said that he wanted to date me exclusively. That's right: He was the one who wanted to take our relationship to the next level. He, who could be dating anyone from, say, twenty-five to fifty-five. I wasn't opposed to dating Steve exclusively; I just hadn't gotten there yet. I was still in my just-dating-casually-because-guys-can't-be-trusted phase. So it took me a little while to get used to his proposal.

Plus it meant I had to give up all my other dates.

I could tell that Steve was serious, and that made him pretty unique in the dating world, for any age. Plus he had so many of my must-haves, none of my non-negotiables, and he possessed the kind of optimism and flexibility that made him seem like a long-term contender. I decided to give it a try, day by day, see how it went.

Now this *was* unusual for me. Typically, once I made up my mind about a guy, I jumped in with both feet and declared love and a future and a joint lease. Of course, that was pre-marriage, pre-kids, pre-divorce. Still, I wondered: Who was this wary woman impersonating me? Whose reluctant heart had taken over my body? Who was this new me who wanted to take things slowly? I'm not sure when I became so cautious, careful, and, to be honest, so cynical, but this was clearly my new speed limit.

I realized that just because we didn't have a plan for our relationship, it didn't mean I couldn't enjoy the ride. I could simply be present and committed and see what unfolded. And over the next several months, I started to recognize myself again. I could sense my heart opening up a little, feeling something close to love, and I didn't rush it.

Steve was definitely different from my ex. Nancy says that's the only kind of men she dates now—the total opposite of who she was married to. Steve's not completely opposite, because my ex has some great qualities, too (yes, they're on my must-haves list). Steve is capable, self-reliant, and he certainly doesn't need saving. That was a huge change for me. It still is: How do I love someone who doesn't need taking care of? I wanted to find out.

> Just because we didn't have a plan for our relationship, it didn't mean I couldn't enjoy the ride.

There are days when I feel this may be my last relationship ever, and there are days that I wonder what in the world I'm

> How do I love
> someone who
> doesn't need
> taking care of?
> I wanted to
> find out.

doing. Once in a while I think I don't want a boyfriend at all, but most of the time I am thrilled to have such a fun, giving man in my life. I worry about the thirteen-year difference; not so much now, but in another ten years when Steve will still be under fifty and I'll be almost sixty. And I don't just wonder about whether he'll want me; I wonder whether I'll want him. Or anyone, for that matter. I mean, I have no idea what menopause will do to me, so I'm concerned about the physical and mental safety of those who will be close to me at the time.

It is clear that I am not the same slightly naïve girl I was when I got married . . . when I thought the most wonderful thing in the world was to have a partner for life. Divorce, and dating after divorce, has changed me. For the better, I'm certain; for the wiser, too. But I'm still working these new perspectives into the old me. Being loved by a man is no longer the all-consuming yearning it was in my twenties and thirties; I'm far more interested in whether or not I can love someone else for a lifetime.

> Being loved by
> a man is no longer
> the all-consuming
> yearning it was in
> my twenties and
> thirties; I'm far
> more interested in
> whether or not I
> can love someone
> else for a lifetime.

So here we are a year later; still on that journey, my prey and I. My friends adore him. He adores me. And yes, I love him fully—sometimes even the way I used to love. Young as he may be, he's smart and he says he knows what he wants: me. Score one for the old lady.

The biggest surprise in this long-term relationship is that I never imagined dating someone who would actually become part of the rest of my life. I honestly thought I would only see him on Wednesday nights and every other weekend. Seriously. I could not picture a holistic relationship.

But Steve has become part of my family—I call it the family of four I always wanted, although it looks a little different from what I had planned: my son, my ex, my boyfriend, and me. You'll often find us all hanging out together at the movies, bowling, or just at home. My friends have taken to calling me Demi.

This friendliness didn't just happen. My ex and I decided to be friends long before we decided to divorce. And it certainly says a lot about the confidence and generosity of both my ex and my boyfriend that we can have the kind of relationship we do. It's certainly good for my son to see that although not everything works out the way we planned it, it doesn't have to be tragic, either. Though I'm sure he'll be lying on a therapist's couch someday whining, "Why couldn't my parents have had a *normal* divorce?"

Our acquaintances think our relationship is a little strange, but we don't really care. Our family thinks it's wonderful (except my dad, who just doesn't get how I can have lunch with my ex and my boyfriend and hug them both good-bye. That's okay: Even though he doesn't understand it, he accepts us). Our friends are getting used to us and are kind of in awe. Believe me, we are not awe inspiring. We're just creative.

Even my friend Stella says it's a little weird when we're all out somewhere and I call, "Honey!" and both my ex and my boyfriend answer. Then again, she's the one who calls them "my two husbands."

I get that I'm really lucky, and that this is pretty unusual. But no one's forcing anyone to be here. This actually works for us. My ex likes Steve and Steve likes my ex and my son likes Steve and my son loves his dad and Steve loves my son, which to me is the most surprising thing of all.

"You love my son?" I ask incredulously, since we are, after all, in the midst of the horrible teenage hormone years. "You didn't even get to see all the good years, before he could talk."

But Steve loves him; he even *likes* him, and my son likes him back. That's just one more thing I couldn't imagine.

And of course, I get to love everyone. It would be nice if my son liked me a little more, but while I can take a stab at dismantling the stereotypical divorce, I am afraid I cannot change thousands of years of adolescence.

Why Do Some Guys Like to Date Older Women?

Something like 35 percent of women over forty are dating younger men. I asked my bevy of young male friends why they like older women, and these are their answers. Try to remember, they're young . . .

Evan says he likes older women because they are confident, and confidence is sexy. They're not needy, they don't ask guys to buy them stuff, and they're not constantly looking for reassurance. He says being with an older woman is freeing—and that freedom enters into all areas of the relationship. Oh, yeah, and he mentioned that older women are typically better in bed.

Jerry says that older women don't have the desperate gotta-get-married, gotta-have-kids thing. He says that in his experience, divorced women with kids aren't even looking to get married, but they are open to a committed relationship with the right guy. He doesn't feel like a prize with a time bomb ticking on it. Oh, and Jerry says the best sex he's ever had is always with older women.

Renaud says that women have to grow into themselves, and that's why older women are more beautiful to him. "They have a sense of self that makes them alluring," he says. And he believes that women are more emotionally advanced then men of the same age. "Men grow smart slowly," Renaud says with a laugh. "Age and experience definitely make a difference in a woman's long-term attractiveness to me."

> "Older women have a sense of self that makes them alluring."

Bill says he loves older women because they have their own friends, jobs, kids, money—they're not dependent on a guy for everything in their lives. A woman who's not always available is a challenge, he says. And we all know about men and their challenge fix.

According to Ryan, older women know who they are, and that allows the men in their lives to be themselves, too. "Older women aren't trying to change us," he says. (That's because we've tried it before and it doesn't work.) And Ryan says it's true that older women are better in bed.

"They take their time, they know what they want, they know how to give, and they are usually up for anything," he explains. "That's just fuckin' sexy."

Really? This is an age thing? Does it have a cap, or will I be even sexier when I'm seventy? It is hard for me to believe that this older-women-are-better is a global comment about all women. Aren't we the same women that men our age are dumping or passing over for younger, needier, less confident, not-as-good-in-bed bimbettes? (And I mean that in the nicest way.)

Nancy says she hears the twenty-something women in her office talking all the time about dating older guys. They tell her that they date men in their thirties and forties because guys their own age can't afford to take them anywhere.

"We're not looking for anything serious, we just want to go out and have fun! And we're not hung up on sex or monogamy or anything like that," a girl who just turned twenty-five told Nancy the other day. What guy could resist that?

But damn it, these girls are messing up the dating ecosystem!

Nancy says she just wants to yell at these girls, "*Stop!* You're ruining it for all the women my age! Now guys in their forties and fifties think they're really something and can have any young thing they want. So they pass right over us."

I say thank God those young girls are passing over the young guys so they can date us, huh?

It probably sounds really dumb, but in my particular situation, so far, age isn't an issue. Steve knows who the Beatles are, he knows what happened to disco, he's seen *The Breakfast Club* and *Rocky* (okay, on video), he doesn't play video games, we watched the same TV shows when we were younger—well, I was in college, he was in grade school. He's been married and divorced; he's been dumped and he's been the dumpee. He's had experiences that many men his age have not. Hell, he's had experiences I haven't had.

I'm youngish (did I hear you say immature?) and he's maturish, and so far it's working for us. Will it work for us in another ten or twenty years? I have no idea. Does anybody know that, whether they are the same age or not? All I know is that age is not in my Manfile, so this beautiful man who embodies nearly everything else that *is* in my Manfile showed up—it's just that he was born when I was learning to shave my legs.

So I consult one of the oldest and wisest women in my life: my mother. She's been married to my dad for fifty-one years and he still makes her laugh. That's the criteria, she says, not age, not even how good they are in bed. This is a little too much information for me—after all, she's my mom—so I ask her what she thinks of my relationship with Steve and our age difference. She says she thinks it's great, which is a little scary, since we rarely agree on the men I date.

"Men usually get old and die before women," my mom says matter-of-factly. "Maybe you won't have to go through that. Maybe you'll actually have someone who can keep up with you and to travel with and have fun with right up until you're . . . well, dead, dear."

To tell you the truth, I think in a different era, my mom would have made one hell of a cougar herself.

In the ~~End~~ Beginning . . . Again

SO HERE WE ARE. THE END. IF YOU'RE ANYTHING LIKE ME, you've come to what you *thought* was the end many times before. Which means you have probably learned, or you may just be learning, that it is not the end at all, but another beginning. Don't you just love do-overs?

I know it's scary. It's awkward. Sometimes it sucks. Believe me, I have nearly died of embarrassment on lots of dates. (Yes, it is a medical fact that you can die from being mortified; where do you think the word *mortician* comes from?)

It's also really, really exciting, because no matter where you are on this journey, you have plenty of company. Good company—brilliant, strong, capable women making daily decisions just like you. We're Googling and JDating and IMing and howling and commiserating. And one thing we've all learned is that *Nothing ever works out exactly how you imagined.* But guess what? We get to keep imagining

> Believe me, I have nearly died of embarrassment on lots of dates.

. . . because just when you believe everything is finished, that will be the beginning. (I'm paraphrasing Louis L'Amour here, but I believe the guy.) I know my Pollyanna-ness makes you want to barf sometimes—me, too. Go ahead. I'll wait. But just because I see the glass as half full doesn't mean it's not true (and it may just be filled with a nice pour of Pinot, you know?)

> Just when you believe everything is finished, that will be the beginning.

I'm not always so perky, don't worry. When I first got divorced, I could never have imagined the place this new road has taken me—even with all the bumps and twists and detours and U-turns and dead ends. (And some surprise attractions along the way, like the cops. Did I ever tell you about the policemen? I think I forgot that one. Probably best. Might get me arrested.)

Our roads may not look the same, but one thing is true for all of us: In order to keep going, you just have to continue putting one foot in front of the other. So I say, why not dress it up in a high-heeled boot and take it one step at a time? It takes courage, I know. It takes a big dose of daring (and a little insanity) to get out there; to like and love and be loved again, especially after you've been through a divorce. But you are braver than you think. (And crazier, too—trust me.)

So here we are, you and I. At a place where we can feel hopeful and happy again. A place where we can define our own rules, shake out our old dreams or create new ones. A place where we were meant to be all along: back on top.

> You are braver than you think. (And crazier, too— trust me.)

And when you do decide to date, I hope to see you out there. If we're online, wink at me, will ya? If we're out, flag me down. I'd like to see your fabulous jeans, give you a hug, wingman you to the cute guy on the other side of the bar.

And buy you a chocolate espresso martini.

Index

Acknowledgments

Without taking myself too seriously, because that would go against every stupid-Ginger-story I ever wrote, I would like to give thanks:

. . . to my Mom and Dad, who married when they were barely old enough to vote and who continue to demonstrate the evolution of a great marriage;

. . . to my brothers and sisters who actually make marriage look pretty easy, so what's my problem? Thank you for laughing with your little sister in all the right places;

. . . to my ex-husband, who consistently shows me that the end of our marriage was, after all, the beginning of a unique and beautiful friendship, and without whom what would I write about?

. . . to my inimitable son, who regularly calls me on my stuff and helps keep me authentic, whether I like it or not; and who, simply by his existence, teaches me the true meaning of unconditional love;

. . . to the angel who is my LLL; sometimes I think I am lying in a coma somewhere and I've just hallucinated this amazing man as some strange extension of myself. Thank you for believing in me, for chuckling even when you'd heard it all before, for showing me so much about my own heart and for letting this relationship unfold;

. . . to Betty, my chosen sister, who believes in me so hard that I feel her from across the Perimeter and who brings me for show-and-tell to all of her other girlfriends;

. . . to Rebecca, whose wit and opinion I respect, and who introduced me to my new best friend; and to Brenda, whose wisdom I depend on and without whom I'd still be just be staring out at the lake—thank you both for reading the early versions and helping me breathe;

. . . to Linda, for the first ten years of fixing me up (and just when you thought it was over. . .) you are always my voice of reason, even though I think you like it better when I have crazy dating stories to tell;

. . . to my soul sisters Page and Anne and The Corporation's Patti and Linda and my lake Girls Night Out girls and all my quippy girlfriends who put up with me and advise me and laugh at me (oops, I mean *with* me); to the fine first four—AB, RB, SS, JS—I could never have stepped out there or gotten back on top without gentlemen like you paving the way;

. . . to my new partners-in-crime, the women and men who shared their first dates, last dates, horror dates, and hilarious dates with me; we really are all in this together, and I could not have written this book without your fun and frankness (well, I could have, but I wouldn't have had such frank and funny and filthy things to say);

. . . to Lara, my editor, who is true and optimistic and smart as hell, and whose original message made me feel like an author and is still on my cell phone ten months later; thank you also to the team at Globe Pequot Press/Morris Publishing for choosing and illustriously illustrating *Back on Top;* to Imee and Laura for having the wisdom to be OCD;

. . . to Nikki Hardin who bulldozes the way for so many of us with her brilliance and originality—thank you for the vote of confidence and the start of everything;

. . . to Debbie Queenan, who first showed me I was a writer (although how she could tell from those early, cringeable stories I'll never know); thank you more than you'll ever know for blowing on the spark;

. . . to Helen, my reader, who is proof that teachers (and fans) come where and when you least expect them;

. . . and to the World for listening and responding (okay, not always with the answers I like to hear) and to God for giving me this particular heart-and-brain combination.

About the Author

GINGER HAS BEEN A FREELANCE WRITER SINCE 1987 when she left IBM in Charlotte, North Carolina, to move to the big city of Atlanta (ostensibly to open her own freelance firm but in truth she had dated all twenty-three of the eligible young Jewish men in the tri-city Mecklenburg area—and fifty-nine of the non-Jewish ones—and needed a bigger pool). She landed a fish in Atlanta, but a few years ago, after thirteen years of marriage and fourteen years of couples therapy, she went on her first post-divorce date and barely lived to tell about it. But tell it she did, and so began her brutally honest, self-revealing, hopefully helpful and hilarious take on dating. With *Back on Top: Fearless Dating After Divorce*, Ginger realizes she isn't doing brain surgery, but that doesn't mean she might not save one or two of us from a date-from-hell. Her goal is that you laugh and hope and learn a little and know that you are not alone. You've always got a girlfriend to share stupid stories with, knowing that she's done stupider.

Ginger is the author of two other books and countless articles and blogs. She spends her time with her family, her son, her ex, her boyfriend, and the absolute best friends a girl could have, especially considering they might someday show up in print.